Ōoka Makoto is a distinguished poet. He is also a major critic of poetry, perhaps the finest in Japan today. For this anthology he has searched through the whole range of Japanese poetry. Janine Beichman has been exceptionally successful in conveying not only the sense but the beauty of the poems and the incisiveness of Mr. Ōoka's remarks.

For some years now the Asahi Shimbun, the leading Japanese newspaper, has carried each day on the front page a poem chosen by Ōoka Makoto along with his comments on its meaning and special interest. The selections he has included in A Poet's Anthology consist not only of haiku, but tanka, linked verse, extracts from poetry written by Japanese in classical Chinese, free verse, and even translations into Japanese of European poems.

Some of the poems are difficult to understand, even for readers who have a general familiarity with the development of Japanese poetry over the centuries, and that is what makes Mr. Ōoka's comments so valuable.

Donald Keene

Publication Supported
by a Grant
from

Z-KAI
ZOSHINKAI
PUBLISHERS, INC.

Through the Association
for
100 Japanese Books

Also from Katydid Books by Mr. Ōoka—

A String Around Autumn, poems

Elegy and Benediction, poems

A Play of Mirrors: Eight Major Poets of Modern Japan, anthology

The Colors of Poetry: Essays on Classic Japanese Verse, criticism

Japanese names are given in the traditional order, family name first.

for Lynn,

A Poet's Anthology

*Hoping this small book
might give you a big
gift, Japanese poetry.*

Makoto

Series

REFLECTIONS

Editor

Thomas Fitzsimmons

A Poet's Anthology
The Range of Japanese Poetry

Ōoka Makoto

Translated by
Janine Beichman

Preface by Donald Keene

KATYDID BOOKS   Sante Fe

KATYDID BOOKS

#1 Balsa Rd., Santa Fe, NM 87505

Translation rights arranged through
Japan Foreign Rights Center

First Edition

Produced by KT DID Productions
Printed in the United States of America on acid-free paper

Distributed by **University of Hawaii Press**
2840 Kolowalu St., Honolulu, HI 96822
FAX: (808) 988-6052

Library of Congress Cataloging in Publication Data

Ōoka Makoto, 1931–
    [Oriori no uta. English]
    A poet's anthology : the range of Japanese poetry / Ōoka Makoto ; translated by Janine Beichman ; preface by Donald Keene.
    p.   cm. — (Reflections ; #3)
    Includes indexes.
    ISBN 0-942668-37-5 : $29.95. — ISBN 0-942668-38-3 (pbk.) : $19.95
    1. Japanese poetry—History and criticism. 2. Seasons in literature. I. Title. II. Series:
Reflections (Rochester, Mich.); #3.
PL727.65.S40613   1993
895.6'1009—dc20   93-35454   CIP

CONTENTS

Introductory

Introductory

Preface

For some years now the *Asahi Shimbun*, the leading Japanese newspaper, has carried each day on the front page a poem chosen by Ōoka Makoto along with his comments on its meaning and special interest. The poems have all been short, necessarily so because of the limited space allotted to the column, but Mr. Ōoka has succeeded in creating an impression of variety and richness by searching through the whole range of Japanese poetry. The selections he has included in *A Poet's Anthology* consist not only of haiku (an obvious choice because of their brevity) but tanka, linked verse, extracts from poetry written by Japanese in classical Chinese, free verse, and even translations into Japanese of European poems.

I cannot think of a newspaper in any other country that gives such prominence to a poetry column. This is a tribute to the *Asahi Shimbun*, but also to its readers, who eagerly scan Mr. Ōoka's column each day and buy the collections of *A Poet's Anthology* that are later published as books. Some of the poems are difficult to understand, even for readers who have a general familiarity with the development of Japanese poetry over the centuries, and that is what makes Mr. Ōoka's comments so valuable. His explanation of the following poem (in free verse) by Tanaka Fuyuji is a good example of how much the reader's appreciation of the poem is likely to be enhanced by his understanding.

Yoru no umi ni tsuriageta kurodai
  Sono me ni shingetsu ga itsu made mo nokotte iru

The poem, in Janine Beichman's translation, is:
  Black bream fished up from the night sea:
  For a long time the new moon remains in its eyes.

The image of the moon still lingering in the eyes of a bream that has
been caught is striking, but on first reading the importance of the
poet's mentioning the new moon might be missed. However, in his
commentary Mr. Ōoka writes, "In reality, the new moon could never
be reflected for hours in the eyes of a bream after it has been caught;
but imagining the sharp, thin shape of the new moon, it comes to
seem possible. Only with a new moon, though: If it were a full moon,
the effect would be ruined."

I think it unlikely that most readers would have caught the special
significance of the words "new moon" if Mr. Ōoka had not called it to
their attention. This has surely been one reason for the popularity of
his column.

As the English translation of the poem and of Mr. Ōoka's commen-
tary indicate, Janine Beichman has been exceptionally successful in
conveying not only the sense but the beauty of the poems and, in the
few words allotted her, the incisiveness of Mr. Ōoka's remarks. These
translations have been a popular feature of every week's Sunday
edition of the *Asahi Evening News*. Because the English version of Mr.
Ōoka's column appears much less often than the daily edition of the
Asahi Shimbun, Ms. Beichman has had to choose from the already
carefully chosen poems those that seem to work best in English. I like
particularly the tanka translations, including this anonymous poem
from the *Kokinshū*:

Ko no ma yori
morikuru tsuki no
kage mireba
kokoro-zukushi no
aki wa kinikeri

When I look up and see
moonlight filter through the trees,
I know that autumn,

heart-exhausting autumn,
is already here.

Her translations of modern tanka, like the following one by
Yamamoto Kaneko, are equally effective:
Kaikō wo
togetaru yume no
ude no naka ni
hikari to narite
ware wa hirogaru

    I dreamt you found me
        at last
     and in your arms
     I turned to light
shed radiance everywhere

In translating this poem, Ms. Beichman has given another dimension
to the expression by the length and placement of the lines, and she has
stressed the modernity of the poem by omitting the normal connective
between the fourth and fifth lines. Among her haiku translations, I
like especially one composed by Iida Dakotsu in 1951:
Iji no te no
kaku mo yawaraka
Aki no kaze

An orphan's hand—
how can it be this soft?
The autumn wind

It is sometimes supposed by readers in the West that the haiku treats
only dragonflies, frogs, sparrows and similar small creatures, but this
poem stabs the reader's heart with its human intensity. As Mr. Ōoka
explains in his commentary, the orphan mentioned in the haiku is the
poet's grandchild; the child's father was killed during the war in
Leyte. The hand is the "infinitely soft hand of a child who never knew

a father." And the autumn wind is lonely.

This haiku is not found in the standard anthologies. I am grateful to Mr. Ōoka for having enabled me to appreciate it, as other readers will undoubtedly be grateful to Janine Beichman for having made it possible for them to read the poems in such effective and moving English.

Donald Keene

New York, 1993

Translator's note

Sometime during the past several years, as I made my weekly translations of *Oriori no Uta*, I came to realize that I was dealing with more than the poetic miscellany the Japanese title so modestly implies. The author's true subtext is the great *variety* of Japanese poetry, its heterogeneity and its inclusiveness. This is why he devotes so much space to such relatively unknown topics as, to give just a few examples, traditional Okinawan poetic forms, eighteenth century satiric verse in both Japanese and Sino-Chinese, and modern women poets. The result is that he expands our notion of the tradition in a way that works against insularity (on the Japanese side) and exoticism (on ours).

This necessarily selective translation cannot do full justice to the original work, but I hope that it gives some idea of its pleasures. My own pleasure in making it has been multiplied many times over by the cooperation so generously given by Ōoka Makoto.

About a hundred collections of poetry are mentioned in the text of this book, but I have translated the Japanese titles only if they work well as English and also add something to the poem being introduced.

In his comments, Ōoka sometimes refers to certain periods in Japanese history and literature. For readers who may not be familiar with them, here is a list, with approximate dates:

Heian	Late 8th-late 12th century
Muromachi	14th-16th century
Tokugawa, or Edo	1603-1868
Meiji	1868-1912
Taishō	1912-1926
Shōwa	1926-1989

A Poet's Anthology

冬が来た。
Fuyu ga kita.

　白い樹樹の光を
　Shiroi kigi no hikari wo

　　体のうちに蓄積しておいて、
　　karada no uchi ni chikuseki shite oite,

　　　夜ふかく眠る
　　　yoru fukaku nemuru

　　　　　前田夕暮
　　　　　Maeda Yūgure

Winter has come.
I pile up
the white light of the trees
in my body,
and sleep deeply at night

Maeda Yūgure started out around 1905, near the end of the Meiji period, as one of the young bloods of the Naturalist tanka, which opposed the romantic style of the tanka poets grouped around the magazine *Myōjō*. Possessed by nature of a temperament keenly sensual, however, he could not stay with the sober palette of realism for long and went through several transformations as he sought his own voice. This colloquial free form tanka, from *Aogashi wa utau* (The Green Oak Sings, 1940), represents one of the important stages in his development.

Now that their leaves have fallen, the winter trees have become brighter and the winter sun shines on them whitely. The poet bundles up the light in his body and sleeps soundly in the black womb of night.

うすらひは
Usurai wa

深山へかへる
miyama e kaeru

花の如
hana no goto

藤田湘子
Fujita Shōshi

Thin ice
like flowers returning
to deep mountains

Fujita Shōshi is a contemporary haiku poet; among his recent collections is *Kariudo* (The Hunter, 1976). This poem appeared in the haiku magazine *Taka* in March 1978.

Thin ice was stretched like a film over the surface of the water, so clear it seemed it would shatter at the touch. The fragile purity must have sent the image of scattering flowers flashing through the author's mind and from there the poem was born. The author completed it with "returning to deep mountains", but the phrase is not susceptible to rational explanation. This poem, with its dependence on the reader's intuitive understanding, is typical of one kind of modern haiku.

篠の葉に
Sasa no ha ni

雪降りつもる
yuki furitsumoru

冬の夜に
fuyu no yo ni

豊の遊びを
toyo no asobi wo

するが愉しさ
suruga tanoshisa

神楽歌
Kagura uta

*Snow falls and piles up on
bamboo leaves*

*It's fun to dance for the gods
on a winter's night*

In ancient times, performances of *kagura*, sacred Shinto dance and song, were often held at court during the winter and thus we have these lyrics.

They contain the only extant usage of the phrase *toyo no asobi*, which is assumed to mean *kagura*. The musicians and singers were divided into two groups, and while one sang the words above the other harmonized with these: "From the time of the gods they danced and sang with bunches of bamboo leaves in their hands."

From ancient times, dancing wildly before the gods was used to reach a state of trance after which, possessed, one danced holding bamboo leaves. The use of bamboo leaves in the lyrics here must be related to that.

いくたびも
Iku tabi mo

雪の深さを
yuki no fukasa wo

尋ねけり
tazunekeri

正岡子規
Masaoka Shiki

Again and again
I ask how high
the snow is

From the 1896 section of *Kanzan Rakuboku* (Cold Mountain, Fallen Trees), a hand-written manuscript left by Masaoka Shiki, father of the modern haiku. One of four haiku entitled "Snow While Sick". "Snow's falling! / I see it through a hole / in the shutter" (*Yuki furu yo Shōji no ana wo mite areba*) is also good, but the one given above is, after all, the best.

In 1896, Shiki's back pain was so severe that he was almost unable to get out of bed. A heavy snow was falling outside, the first in a long time, and while imagining what it looked like as it piled up, Shiki asked his mother and young sister, who looked after him, how high it was again and again. The compressed syntax of haiku is able to express with poignant intensity the invalid's excitement, imagination and yearning.

口中一顆の
kōchū ikka no

霰を啄み
hyō wo tsuibami

火の鳥や
hi no tori ya

三橋鷹女
Mitsuhashi Takajo

A hailstone held
in its beak,
the firebird soars

From *Mitsuhashi Takajo Zenkushū* (Collected Haiku of Mitsuhashi Takajo, 1976).

Where is the firebird flying? It flies in the poet's heart. And it holds in its beak a single hailstone, against whose glittering ice the flames that engulf the bird increase in brightness. Cold, yet hot, a bird in a woman's dream.

Takajo died in 1972 at the age of seventy-three. Defying the conventional script for a woman's life until the end, she wrote many poems like this, romantic and touchingly courageous self-portraits.

冬ざれや
Fuyuzare ya

ものを言ひしは
Mono wo iishi wa

籠の鳥
kago no tori

高橋淡路女
Takahashi Awajijo

Winter desolation
What speaks is
the caged bird

From *Kaji no Ha* (The Mulberry Leaf, 1937). Takahashi Awajijo was a haiku poet born in Kobe; she died in 1955, at the age of sixty-four. She joined the women's branch of the Hototogisu Haiku Association in 1916 and later studied haiku under Iida Dakotsu. She is said to have particularly liked the haiku of the Edo period poets Matsuo Bashō and Yosa Buson and their influence can be seen in the elegance of her diction.

On a desolate winter day, in the hushed quiet of someone's house, a bird, perhaps a mynah, speaks out from time to time. Its mistress has no one to talk to; beyond the bird, there is only silence.

The author was widowed early and brought up her only child alone, never remarrying.

中原よ。
Nakahara yo.

地球は冬で寒くて暗い。
Chikyū wa fuyu de samukute kurai.

ぢゃ。
Ja.

さやうなら。
Sayōnara.

草野心平
Kusano Shinpei

Nakahara, friend!
The earth is wintry, cold and dark.
Well then, good-bye.

From *Zekkei* (Beautiful View, 1940), this is the poem *"Kūkan"* (Space), in its entirety.

The poet Nakahara Chūya died in October 23, 1937, at the age of thirty. Shinpei wrote "Space" in memory of him but it was not published until April 1939, in the sixth issue of *Rekitei*. Probably this was because there was a two and a half year hiatus between the fifth and sixth issues of the magazine, which was then Shinpei's only venue of publication.

As a boy, I read this poem in some anthology and have a vivid memory of my excitement at realizing for the first time how much poetry could convey with just a few words.

海暮れて
Umi kurete

鴨の声
kamo no koe

ほのかに白し
honoka ni shiroshi

松尾芭蕉
Matsuo Bashō

The waters fade
and the wild ducks' cries
are faintly white

Matsuo Bashō was a popular haiku poet with a flourishing career when he left Edo on the journey recorded in the travel diary *Nozarashi Kikō* (Wind-Washed Skull Journey, 1684). It was to prove a memorable journey, which established the Bashō style of haiku in Nagoya and Atsuta, and gave birth to the linked verse collection *Fuyu no Hi* (A Winter's Day).

This haiku was written during Bashō's stay near Nagoya in Owari. He had, he recorded, spent the whole day by the sea. The cries of the wild ducks spread over the pitchblack surface of the water — faintly white, it seemed, in the darkness.

The word *shiroshi* (white, 白し) must also mean *shirushi* (distinct, bright, 顕し). And yet, it is, paradoxically, a "faint" whiteness, a "faint" brightness.

Haiku are, of course, usually seventeen syllables and this is no exception. In its manner of division, however, it is unusual, being divided into 5-5-7 syllables instead of the conventional 5-7-5. Read slowly, with slight pauses between each line, the Japanese gives an effect of hushed stillness.

家毎に
Ie goto ni

柿吊るし干す
kaki tsurushi hosu

高木村
Takagi-mura

住み古りにけり
sumifurinikeri

夢のごとくに
yume no gotoku ni

久保田不二子
Kubota Fujiko

From every house
persimmons hung to dry
I've lived for ages
in Takagi Village
as if in a dream

From *Niwa Suzume* (Garden Sparrows, 1952). A tanka poet born in Takagi, Shimo Suwa, Nagano Prefecture, Fujiko died in 1965 at age 79. Married to Kubota Toshihiko, her father's adopted son, who was later known as the tanka poet Shimagi Akahiko, she joined the tanka group Araragi, and came to Tokyo with her husband. But they later returned to Takagi, where her husband died of illness. She spent most of her life in Takagi.

Persimmons hung out to dry are a beautiful sight in mountain villages from late autumn to early winter. This poem has a quiet, tranquil tone. The author must have had a special feeling for persimmons. One of her husband's pen names was "Man of Persimmon Village" and the title of his last volume of tanka means "Persimmon Shadows".

枯蘆に
Kareashi ni

曇れば水の
kumoreba mizu no

眠りけり
nemurikeri

阿部みどり女
Abe Midorijo

By withered reeds
dimmed by clouds,
the water sleeps

From *Bifū* (Breezes, 1955). A haiku poet born in Sapporo, Midorijo died in 1980 at age 93. She began to write in the early Taishō period. As part of her effort to perfect the "sketch from life" style advocated by Takahama Kyoshi, she studied drawing with Morita Tsunetomo and qualified six times in succession for the prestigious Shunyō Society of Art Exhibition.

Few women were as capable as Midorijo of expressing passion and elegance in the deliberately understated "sketch from life" style. Water is sleeping lightly beneath the withered reeds on a cloudy day. Just a simple description, but somehow it evokes a world of great depth.

吏の田を撿しに来れば
Ri no den wo kenshi ni kitareba

連日里正が宅に
renjitsu risei ga taku ni

珍羞は厨に満ちて堆し
chinshū wa kuriya ni michite uzutakashi

菅 茶山
Kan Chazan

The official is here inspecting rice
and every day in the headman's house
delicacies fill the kitchen, piled high

From *Kōyō Sekiyō Sonsha Shi* (Poems of Autumn Leaves, Evening Sun, and Village Houses). A leading poet of Chinese verse in the late Edo Period. Quoted here are the last three lines of a *gogon zekku* poem (4 lines, each 5 characters) titled "Taken Down from the Words of Passersby on a Road in Bitchū." Chazan recorded without change the excited talk of villagers on a street in Bitchū as they gossiped about the official's visit and the fancy treatment he was getting from the village headman. Banquets and bribes to butter up our betters: one of those styles of life that knows no season.

耳
Mimi

私の耳は貝のから
Watashi no mimi wa kai no kara

海の響をなつかしむ
umi no hibiki wo natsukashimu

堀口大学訳
ジャン・コクトー作
Horiguchi Daigaku's translation of
Jean Cocteau

Ears

My ears are seashells
They remember the ocean's echoes

From *Gekka no Ichigun* (A Gathering Beneath the Moon, 1925). This collection of translations sent shock waves through the world of poetry and inspired the new generation of Shōwa period poets. In addition to 19th century European and American poets already known from the Meiji period, it introduced many new 20th century poets, especially French ones, including Cocteau, whose "Ears" won great popularity.

The coincidence in form between ears and seashells opens a door to the wide sea. The natural beauty and grace of the Japanese makes the reader forget it is a translation.

をみなにて
Omina ni te

またも来む世ぞ
matamo komuyo zo

生れまし
umaremashi

花もなつかし
Hana mo natsukashi

月もなつかし
Tsuki mo natsukashi

山川登美子
Yamakawa Tomiko

Let me be born
a woman again
in the world to come
And I will love the flowers
And I will love the moon

From *Yamakawa Tomiko*, Vol. 17 of *Gendai Tanka Zenshū* (Complete Modern Tanka, 1929). After yielding her teacher Yosano Tekkan, whom she loved, to Hō Akiko, Tomiko married a man chosen by her parents. Soon widowed, she returned to the *Myōjō* poets' circle, where she exercised her literary talent to the full for a brief period, and then died of tuberculosis at the age of 30. No one would call the last half of her life very happy, but, with a presentiment of the death that would soon claim her, she wrote that she wanted to be born a woman again in her next life. "And I will love the flowers / And I will love the moon"—a tone so intense that there is no room to ask for reasons.

白鳥は
Shiratori wa

哀しからずや
kanashikarazu ya

空の青
Sora no ao

海のあをにも
umi no ao ni mo

染まずただよふ
somazu tadayou

若山牧水
Wakayama Bokusui

White bird,
are you not sad?
You drift, never dyed
by the blue of the sea
or the sky's azure

From *Umi no Koe* (Sea Voices, 1908), Bokusui's first volume of tanka, published privately the year he graduated from the English Literature Department of Waseda University. The famous poem beginning "*Iku yamakawa*" (How many mountains and rivers) is in the same volume.

"White bird" means a seagull here. The cover illustration by Hirafuku Hyakusui must have been based on this poem. Contrasting the white of the bird to the blue of the sea and sky, the poet grieves over the bird, alive in the midst of nature's vastness, and over his own youthful loneliness. Contemporary tanka poets avoid repetitions like "*sora no ao umi no ao*" (literally, "the blue of the sky, the blue of the sea"*) but in Bokusui's poems they work wonderfully to express feeling.

* Translated as "blue" and "azure" because of the shift from *kanji* to *hiragana*.—Tr.

老いたるは
Oitaru wa

皆かしこかり
mina kashikokari

この国に
Kono kuni ni

身を殺す者
mi wo korosu mono

すべて若人
subete wakōdo

与謝野　寛（鉄幹）
Yosano Hiroshi (Tekkan)

The old men
are all so wise
In this country
it is always the young
who sacrifice their lives

From *Kashi no Ha* (Oak Leaves, 1910), a collection of modern-style poems and tanka. One of six tanka lamenting the accidental deaths of the crew of Submarine No. 6, shipwrecked in the waters off Shinminato in Yamaguchi Prefecture, on April 15, 1910. The captain, Lt. Junior Grade Sakuma Tsutomu, continued to write his log up until the moment he died, and his composure and bravery were greatly praised. Hiroshi mourns his martyrdom, repudiates war, and indicts the "old men" who in their "wisdom" send the young into the maw of death while living on themselves.

Hiroshi wrote several tanka and modern-style poems in this vein and they deserve more attention than they have been given until now.

佐保神の
Saogami no

別れかなしも
wakare kanashi mo

来ん春に
Kon haru ni

ふたゝび逢はん
futatabi awan

われならなくに
ware naranaku ni

正岡子規
Masaoka Shiki

Ah sad, this parting
from Lady Sao
In the spring to come
how can I hope
to meet her again

From *Take no Sato Uta* (Poems from the Bamboo Village, 1904). Written at the beginning of May, 1901, this is one of the most beautiful poems of Shiki's last years. For six years, due to tuberculosis and spinal decay, he had been confined to bed, doing virtually nothing but write.

Saogami is *Saohime,* the goddess of spring. *Saogami no wakare* is the parting from spring. *Ware naranaku ni* is literally an emphatic way of saying, "it will not be me." He thinks wistfully that he is now so ill he may never meet the goddess of spring again.

Shiki loved spring. He did live on through spring of the following year, but died in the early autumn, on September 19, 1902.

闘鶏の
Tōkei no

眼つむれて
manako tsumurete

飼はれけり
kawarekeri

村上鬼城
Murakami Kijō

A fighting cock,
eyes gone, still kept,
still fed

From *Kijō Kushū* (Kijō's Haiku, 1926).
Born into a high-ranking samurai family,
he contracted ear disease and for many
years worked as a poorly paid scribe at the
Takasaki District Court in order to sup-
port his wife and 10 children. He studied
haiku with the young Masaoka Shiki and
then Takahama Kyoshi.

In his style, Kijō confronted life head on
and showed a rugged individuality. A
blinded fighting cock is of no use any-
more. One would expect it to be killed, but
out of pity, its owner still keeps it. The
poet sees himself in the rooster but avoids
sentimentality by letting only the rooster
into the poem.

わが家は
Waga ie wa

がらくたばかり
garakuta bakari

がらくたの
Garakuta no

一部ぞわれも
ichibu zo ware mo

子も妻もまた
ko mo tsuma mo mata

筏井嘉一
Ikadai Kaichi

Rubbish—that's my house,
nothing but rubbish,
even me
And my wife,
and my children, too

From *Aratae* (Rough Cloth, 1940). A tanka poet from Takaoka City, Kaichi died in 1971, at the age of 71. He worked as an elementary school music teacher until he was quite old. As a resident of downtown Tokyo for many years, he created his own unique world, depicting in poems the poverty, pain and sadness of urban life among the lower classes. He often wrote about his students, as in the poem: "At night / the girl dances / to support her family / and in her classes in the day / spends her time napping." One of his pupils engaged in prostitution to help her family; that kind of harsh life, common in the prewar era, lies in the background of this poem.

The decade of 1935-1945, not so long ago in years, has become part of the distant past.

鉦鳴らし
Kane narashi

信濃の国を
Shinano no kuni wo

行き行かば
yuki yukaba

ありしながらの
arishi nagara no

母見るらむか
haha miruramu ka

窪田空穂
Kubota Utsubo

As I go about
the land of Shinano
ringing my pilgrim's bell,
will I see, perhaps,
my mother as she was then?

From *Mahiru No* (The Fields at High Noon, 1905). Born in the outskirts of Matsumoto in the Shinshū district, Utsubo was the last child, born when his mother was past 40, and especially loved by his parents; but he lost his mother, and then his father, while still a boy.

Kane narashi means "becoming a pilgrim." *Haha miruramu ka* can be interpreted as "will my mother perhaps see me?" but the author seems to have meant "will I be able to see my mother?" He has, that is, omitted the "*wo*" between *haha* and *miru-ramu*, and also between *kane* and *narashi*.

This has been one of the most popular poems about filial love, and may even have influenced the well-known tanka by Wakayama Bokusui that begins, "How many mountains and rivers must I cross..."

山ふかみ
Yama fukami

春とも知らぬ
haru to mo shiranu

松の戸に
matsu no to ni

たえだえかかる
taedae kakaru

雪の玉水
yuki no tamamizu

式子内親王
Shikishi Naishinnō

Deep in the mountains,
too deep to know of spring,
sparkling beads of melted snow
fall slowly, drop by drop,
on my pine bough door

Shinkokinshū (13[th]c.), Book 1, Spring.

A cottage in the mountains at the beginning of spring. So deep in the mountains that one cannot imagine spring has come ─ and yet, drops of snow melted by the sun are falling slowly on the rough door made of pine boughs and boards.

Shinkokinshū poets had a fondness for pictorial beauty and one sees it here in the juxtaposition of the pines' green and the sparkling drops of melted snow. With the loneliness of the mountain cottage enfolded in the luster and brightness of "sparkling beads", another layer is added to the taste of spring.

月の輝くは
Tsuki no kagayaku wa

晴れたる雪の如し
haretaru yuki no gotoshi

梅花は
Baika wa

照れる星に似たり
tereru hoshi ni nitari

菅原道真
Sugawara no Michizane

The moon sparkles like new fallen snow
The plum blossoms resemble shining stars

The first two lines of "A View of Plum Blossoms on a Spring Night", the first poem in Michizane's collection of Chinese poetry, *Kanke Bunsō*. The collection is ordered by year of composition, so this is Michizane's first poem, written at the age of 11 (10 by modern count). It is thought that his tutors were his father Koreyoshi and his father's disciple Shimada Tadaomi. The third and fourth lines read "How lovely! In the garden where the golden mirror sheds its light, / clusters of plum blossoms like white jewels give off scent."

An artless poem, it gives an impression of freshness and is early evidence of Michizane's great talent.

ゆふめしに
Yūmeshi ni

かますご喰へば
kamasugo kueba

風薫
kaze kaoru

凡兆
Bonchō

蛭の口処を
Hiru no kuchido wo

かきて気味よき
kakite kimi yoki

芭蕉
Bashō

Sand eels
for dinner, and the
fragrant wind

Scratching that leech bite
feels so good

From "The Ash-water Bucket" sequence of *The Monkey's Raincoat*, one of the *haikai* linked-verse collections of Bashō and his followers. The two verses describe a man sitting down to dinner after hard manual labor in the rice paddies and scratching to his heart's content at the place where a leech sucked his blood.

Kamasugo is *ikanago*, sand eel, not the larger *kamasu*, saury-pike. *Kaze kaoru*, fragrant wind, is a summer season word which captures the special freshness of summer breezes that come from the southeast.

The feeling of relief at sitting down to a simple dinner after a full day's work is vividly conveyed by the pleasurable scratching of an itch.

天の海に
Ame no umi ni

雲の波立ち
kumo no nami tachi

月の船
tsuki no fune

星の林に
hoshi no hayashi ni

漕ぎ隠る見ゆ
kogikakuru miyu

柿本人麻呂歌集
Kakinomoto no Hitomaro Kashū

In the sea of heaven
cloud waves rise
and the moon boat sails
into a forest of stars,
to be seen no more

The first poem of Book 7, Miscellaneous Poems, of the *Man'yōshū* (8th c.).

Heaven is a vast sea, and the clouds floating in it are high, foaming waves. The moon, a boat, crosses them, and disappears into a forest of stars. Of the many beautiful descriptive poems in the *Man' yōshū* this is one of the more unusual. I like the metaphor "a forest of stars."

Someone in ancient times may have looked at the moon boat crossing the heavenly sea and fantasized something like a UFO, come from a far-off star.

天に鳴響む大主
Ame ni toyomu ōnushi

明けもどろの花の
ake modoro no hana no

咲い渡り
saiwatari

あれよ　見れよ　清らやよ
Are yo Mire yo Kiyoraya yo

地天とよむ大ぬし
Jiten toyomu ōnushi

おもろさうし
Omoro Sōshi

*The Great Lord echoes
through the heavens,
a blazing red flower in full bloom
There, look there! How bright!
The Great Lord resounds
through earth and sky*

The 22 volume *Omoro Sōshi* is a collection of poetry and song of the Okinawa and Amami archipelagoes, dating from about the 12th century to the early 17th.

The *omoro* is a sacred song of prayer to the gods for the prosperity and good harvests of a village community. Varied in content and form, it is Okinawa's oldest kind of poetry, and occupies an important position in the history of Japanese literature.

Modoro, blazing, means to burn so brightly the shape is blurred. This poem is a hymn of praise to the morning sun, sublime in its vision of the rising sun as a gigantic flower.

思ひ有明の
ウムイアリアキヌ
Umui ariaki nu

夜半のつれなさや
ユワヌツィリナサヤ
yuwa nu tsirinasa ya

なれぬよそ島に
ナリヌユスジマニ
Narinu yusuijima ni

をてど知ゆる
ヲゥティドゥシユル
outidu shiyuru

仲間節・よみ人しらず
Nakamabushi, yomibito shirazu

The pain of longing through the night,
until the dying moon !
I knew it first
in a distant land, far from home
       Nakama song, Anonymous

Ryūka Zenshū (Complete Ryūka Collection, 1968). The *ryūka* is the tanka of Okinawa. While the *omoro* is a narrative form, the *ryūka* is a lyrical one, most often about love. Authorship is diverse. There are 30 syllables, arranged 8-8-8-6, and it was sung to samisen accompaniment. It entered Yamato together with the samisen, and had a great influence on the development of pre-modern song, which is based on a 7-7-7-5 form.

面影ばかりのこして
Omokage bakari nokoshite

あづまのかたへくだりし人の名は
Azuma no kata e kudarishi hito no na wa

しらじらといふまじ
shirajira to iumaji

閑吟集
Kanginshū

Memories were all he left behind
when he went down to the East,
and never ever will I tell his name

A poem like a sigh that escaped a woman left behind when her man set off for the Eastern provinces, this is a good example of the sophistication of pre-modern song. The compression of the first line is especially fine. *Shirajira* means openly, but also suggests *shiranai*, I don't know (his name). I will never speak his name, will hide it forever in my heart, she vows.

It's interesting to compare this man who went down to the East to a sad wanderer like the ancient poet Ariwara no Narihira.

ゆふぐれは
Yūgure wa

雲のはたてに
kumo no hatate ni

ものぞ思ふ
mono zo omou

天つ空なる
Amatsu sora naru

人をこふとて
hito wo kou tote

よみ人しらず
Yomibito shirazu

When evening falls,
my reveries turn
to the farthest clouds,
for I love one who dwells
in the vast skies above
                    Anonymous

Kokinshū (early 10ᵗʰc.), Book 11, Miscellaneous Poems. *Kumo no hatate ni* means to the end of the clouds. *Amatsu sora naru hito* means a person in the sky above, that is, a person one loves but who is impossibly far above one in rank. The speaker is probably male, and the object of his affections a woman of such high rank that, under the prevailing social system, he could never win her. The poem, however, transcends such realistic circumstances and expresses the longing and anguish common to all who love.

This poem has enjoyed wide popularity, and is the prototype of poems about the melancholy, unrequited lover gazing at the sky.

あやにくに
Ayaniku ni

煩ふ妹が
wazurau imo ga

夕ながめ
yū nagame

越人
Etsujin

A girl
sick with love
gazes at the twilit sky

あの雲はたが
Ano kumo wa ta ga

なみだつつむぞ
namida tsutsumu zo

芭蕉
Bashō

Whose tears
do those clouds enfold?

From "Wild Geese" a sequence in *Wild Fields*, one of the Bashō linked-verse collections. It is as if the classical world of the preceding poem was reborn in linked verse

Ayaniku means unfortunately. *Wazurau* means sick, but here implies love-sickness. *Yū nagame* is a tormented heart gazing vacantly at the twilit sky.

The verse which Bashō added to Etsujin's asks whose are the tears held within the clouds of the evening sky, thus apprehending the woman's anguish as part of a larger landscape, and adding a dramatic touch.

もの思へば
Mono omoeba

沢の螢も
sawa no hotaru mo

わが身より
wagami yori

あくがれ出づる
akugare izuru

魂かとぞ見る
tama ka to zo miru

和泉式部
Izumi Shikibu

Sunk in reverie
I seem to see
in the river fireflies
my soul
gone forth in longing
from my body

Goshūishū (11th c.), Miscellaneous Poems. The prefatory note says that Shikibu composed this poem while watching the fireflies fly over Mitarashi River during a retreat at Kibune Shrine in Kurama, after her lover had forsaken her.

It was believed that the body and the soul were originally separate, and that the soul split off at times of great sadness, as here, *akugare*, in longing. Sunk in grief, even the flickering light of the fireflies in the darkness looks like her own soul strayed from her body. The poem's inspiration may have been fear, but the tone is wonderfully strong, almost voluptuous.

The god of the shrine is said to have replied: "Do not grieve so long / that your soul becomes like / the spray flying off / from the foaming rapids / as they cascade through remote mountains." (*Okuyama ni tagirite otsuru takitsuse no tama chiru bakari mono na omohi so*).

夜の海に釣りあげた黒鯛
Yoru no umi ni tsuriageta kurodai

その眼に新月がいつまでものこっている
Sono me ni shingetsu ga itsu made mo nokotte iru

田中冬二
Tanaka Fuyuji

Black bream fished up from the night sea:
For a long time the new moon remains in its eyes

From the free verse collection *Budō no Onna* (Woman of Grapes, 1966), the poem *Shingetsu* (New Moon) in its entirety.

Tanaka was a free verse poet who died in 1980 at the age of 85. Many readers were devoted to him because of his precise observation of seasonal sights all over Japan and the refined and elegant simplicity of his diction.

In reality, the new moon could never be reflected for hours in the eyes of a bream after it has been caught; but imagining the sharp, thin shape of the new moon, it comes to seem possible. Only with the new moon, though: If it were a full moon, the effect would be ruined.

あけびの実は汝の霊魂の如く
Akebi no mi wa nanji no reikon no gotoku
夏中ぶらさがってゐる
natsujū burasagatte iru

西脇順三郎
Nishiwaki Junzaburō

Akebia fruits, like your soul,

dangle the summer long

From the free verse collection, *Ambarvalia*, 1933. Nishiwaki died in 1982, age 88.

This is the last two lines of the eight-line poem *Tabibito*. The subject is a contemporary traveller roaming ancient Europe; the first, startling line, is the apostrophe: "You, ill-tempered traveller!" (*Nanji kanshakumochi no tabibito yo*). The two lines above follow these: "Return to your village. / Bless the cliffs of your birthplace! / Their naked earth is your dawn." (*Nanji wa nanji no mura e kaere Kyōri no gake wo shukufuku seyo Sono hadaka no tsuchi wa nanji no yoake da*).

Pale purple akebia fruit: a strangely alluring vision of the poet's own soul dangling in the hills, with a restless nostalgia for the eternal.

水鳥の
Mizutori no

背に残りゐる
se ni nokori iru

夕明り
yū akari

湖暮れゆけば
umi kureyukeba

ただ仄かなる
tada honoka naru

大岡　博
Ōoka Hiroshi

*Evening light lingers
on the wild ducks' backs,
then, as the lake
darkens,
grows pale*

From *Keiryū* (Mountain Streams, 1952). Ōoka was a tanka poet who died in 1981, age 74. He studied poetry under Kubota Utsubo. *Mountain Streams* was his first tanka collection; this, written in 1932, its first poem.

At Lake Ashinoko, in the Hakone mountains, the sun sinks behind the hills. The last, thin light rests faintly on the ducks' backs, felt, almost, rather than seen.

The pale light of the outer world may actually be a twilight time within the young poet himself. He was my father, 25 then; I was one year old. I often reread this poem of my father's youth.

あなたは勝つ
Anata wa katsu

ものとおもつて
mono to omotte

ゐましたかと
imashita ka to

老いたる妻の
oitaru tsuma no

さびしげにいふ
sabishige ni iu

土岐善麿
Toki Zenmaro

*'Did you think
we'd win?'
said
my old wife
sadly*

From *Natsukusa* (Summer Grass, 1946). Zenmaro was a tanka poet who died on April 15, 1980, aged 94. All his life he pursued broad intellectual activities and literary projects, never content to stay within the narrow borders of the tanka world.

This poem records verbatim a conversation with his wife in 1945, shortly after the war ended with Japan's defeat. It sounds like simple prose, but I feel that among the many poems from those days this is one of the best. After it comes this: "Three sons / drafted, gone to war. / Should I have prayed / for them / to lose it?" The same thought was shared by many parents.

炎天の
Enten no

遠き帆やわが
tōki ho ya Waga

心の帆
kokoro no ho

山口誓子
Yamaguchi Seishi

Distant sail
under blazing sun, sail
of my heart

From *Ensei* (Distant Star, 1947). Seishi, born 1901 in Kyoto, is one of the most respected haiku poets today.

Depending on one's point of view, one might call this either a poem of youth, in which a young person expresses longing, or else a poem of maturity, in which an older person's sense of regret and isolation is projected onto a sail seen far off in the distance. The brief haiku form, rather than conveying its creator's real meaning openly, sometimes, as here, shows us a strangely beautiful world, beyond time, beyond thought.

In actual fact, this poem was written on August 22, 1945, one week after the end of the war, while Seishi was convalescing from illness near the sea at Ise. "Down and out" would probably best describe the mood it was born from.

逸りきて
Hayari kite

けやき大樹に
keyaki taiju ni

こもるかぜ
komoru kaze

非命の魂の
himei no tama no

万の鈴音
man no suzu oto

山田あき
Yamada Aki

Impetuously the wind
breezes in, then rests
in the great zelkovas,
its whispers the hand bells
of 10,000 souls
lost in war

From *Sanga Mugen* (Infinite Mountains and Rivers, 1977). This female poet's works do not have a clear and easy flow. Even near 80, her poems often had a kind of uncompromising quality, as though she had simply held her breath and let loose with what was on her mind.

At the height of summer, when a gust of wind comes to rest among the large zelkova trees, the whispering of the leaves is like a multitude of hand bells rung by the souls of those "untimely dead" (*himei*) who perished in the fires of war.

木のまより
Ko no ma yori

もりくる月の
morikuru tsuki no

影見れば
kage mireba

心づくしの
kokoro-zukushi no

秋は来にけり
aki wa kinikeri

よみ人しらず
Yomibito shirazu

When I look up and see
moonlight filter through the trees,
I know that autumn,
heart-exhausting autumn,
is already here

Kokinshū, Autumn. *Kokorozukushi* means to use up one's heart, exhaust one's feelings. With autumn, the scenery of the fields and mountains changes. Here and there beautiful reds and yellows begin to dot the natural world. But this is a golden light that lasts but an instant and then is gone. Every time I think of it, says the poet, my heart is uneasy.

The poem's center is this subjective feeling, but at the same time its evocative language objectively captures, at some primal level, the atmosphere of autumn. It was this that made it popular, and widely quoted, in *The Tale of Genji* and elsewhere.

秋風や
Akikaze ya

しらきの弓に
Shiraki no yumi ni

弦はらん
tsuru haran

向井去来
Mukai Kyorai

Autumn breeze—
Come, string a bow of
unvarnished wood!

An autumn poem from *Wild Fields*.

Kyorai was one of Bashō's closest disciples. Elegant, genteel, and also hardworking, he was accomplished in the martial arts. A bow of unvarnished wood, not even bound in rattan — to its whiteness, fresh as the autumn breeze, he attaches a bowstring, and with intense pleasure aims straight at the target.

In part because it hints at the author's own personality, this became one of Kyorai's best known poems. When Natsume Sōseki taught high school in Kumamoto, Terada Torahiko, then his student but later to become a scientist and member of Sōseki's literary circle, asked advice on how to compose haiku. Sōseki gave this poem as an example of what the beginner should strive for.

空をあゆむ
Sora wo ayumu

朗朗と月ひとり
rō-rō to tsuki hitori

荻原井泉水
Ogiwara Seisensui

It walks the sky, cloudless,
clear: the moon alone

From *Gensen* (The Wellspring, 1960). Seisensui, a haiku poet born in Tokyo, died in 1976, age 91. In 1911, with his haiku teacher Kawahigashi Hekigotō, he began the magazine *Sōun*, for publishing New Tendency haiku. Some years later, he shifted to free-form haiku and nurtured the talent of such poets as Ozaki Hōsai and Taneda Santōka. He was extremely prolific, publishing about 400 volumes of verse and prose.

This poem dates from 1920. The moon is alone. So am I. And so we walk together, one above and one below, in freedom, bright and clear. *Rō-rō*, translated as "cloudless, clear", is where the poem's emphasis lies.

心の澄むものは
Kokoro no sumu mono wa

秋は山田の庵毎に
aki wa yamada no io-goto ni

鹿驚かすてふ引板の声
shika odorokasu chō hita no koe

衣しで打つ槌の音
koromo shide utsu tsuchi no oto

梁塵秘抄
Ryōjin Hishō

Autumn lifts up the heart with these:
The voice of deer-scaring clappers
from every hut in the mountain fields
The sound of mallets, beating on against silk

An example of a medieval song based on a list. To scare away the deer and boars that lay waste to mountain crops, clappers were strung on ropes from the huts set up in the fields during the growing season. Their sound, and that of the fulling of silk (to bring out the gloss) brought peace to the heart.

Shide utsu: two people beat in turn, so there is no pause between strikes. Another interpretation takes it as beating gently, but since it is coupled with the sound of clappers, it seems more appropriate to take it as a loud and clear sound echoing through the clear autumn evening.

吹きしをる
Fukishioru

四方の草木の
yomo no kusaki no

うら葉見えて
uraba miete

風にしらめる
kaze ni shirameru

秋のあけぼの
aki no akebono

永福門院内侍
Eifuku Mon'in no Naishi

All green things and trees
blown and bent,
the back leaves shine
white in the wind,
in autumn's dawn
Lady-in-waiting of Eifuku Mon'in

Gyokuyōshū (early 14ᵗʰc.), Autumn. Daughter of Fujiwara Motosuke, a high-ranking noble, and lady-in-waiting to Emperor Fushimi's consort Eifuku Mon'in, this poet participated in the development of the new style associated with the *Gyokuyō-shu* and *Fūgashū* (mid-14ᵗʰc.).

Shioru: the way wind and snow push plants down. *Uraba* means the top leaves, but here seems to denote the undersides of the leaves as well, exposed when they are bent by the wind.

The autumn day dawns amidst the noisy rustling of leaves. White leaves, the whiteness of the lightening sky: each in motion, changing moment by moment.

赤とんぼ
Akatonbo

　まだ恋とげぬ
　mada koi togenu

　　朱さやか
　　ake sayaka

　　　佐野青陽人
　　　Sano Seiyōjin

Red dragonfly,
its love not yet fulfilled:
Scarlet bright

From *Ama no Kawa* (The Milky Way, 1941). A haiku poet born in Takaoka, Toyama Prefecture, Seiyōjin died in 1963, age 67. He belonged to the group of poets that followed Watanabe Suiha. In addition to working for a trading firm run by Americans (his pen name *Seiyōjin* 青陽人, "blue sun man," is homonymous with 西洋人, "Occidental man"), he studied Noh performance for many years and at one time even taught Noh singing.

Seiyōjin's family had been dyers for generations and one senses in his polished style the careful craftsmanship of the artisan. One of his best known works is: "Look! The Milky Way / Now I see clearly / the bottom of the storm" (*Ama no kawa ōkaze no soko akiraka ni*). With the same sure art, the poem here captures the throb of life in a living creature.

金烏西舎に臨らひ
Kin'u seisha ni terai

鼓声短命を催す
Kosei tanmei wo unagasu

泉路賓主無し
Senro hinshu nashi

此の夕家を離りて向かふ
Kono yūbe ie wo sakarite mukau

大津皇子
Ōtsu no Miko

The golden crow lights the houses in the west
And drumbeats hurry my short life on
There are no hosts or guests on the road to
death:
Tonight I leave my home, to venture there

From the 8th century *Kaifūsō*, the oldest extant collection of Chinese verse made in Japan. The author, son of Emperor Tenmu, was gifted in the arts of peace and war, with a special talent for poetry. After the death of his father, he was one of the leading contenders for the kingship, but was executed on suspicion of fomenting rebellion.

This poem was written on the day of his own death. *Kin'u,* "golden crow," is the sun. The sun sets, its light spreading west, and the drum that announces night echoes as though further hastening the end of his short life. There are no companions on the road to death, "no hosts or guests." Alone, he leaves his home and sets off on that distant journey.

茨小木の下には
Ubara kogi no shita ni wa

鼬鼠笛吹く
itachi fue fuku

猿奏づ
Saru kanazu

稲子丸は拍子打つ
Inagomaro wa hyōshi utsu

蟋蟀は鉦鼓打つ
Kirigirisu wa shōgo utsu

風俗歌
Fuzoku-uta

Beneath the brier bush,
Weasel plays the whistle.
Monkey dances to
Mr. Locust's beat
and Cricket strikes the bell.

Fuzoku-uta were provincial folksongs from the Heian period and earlier which were often sung at banquets in the homes of nobles. Only about fifty are extant today. Some are close to tanka in form, while others are one of a kind. The one here, from the *Taigenshō*, describes an orchestra of small animals reminiscent of the medieval picture scroll *Chōjū Giga* (Carnival of Bird and Beast) attributed to the artist-priest Toba Sōjō. The Heian period anthology *Ryōjin Hishō* has a similar song.

獏のすむ
Baku no sumu

野辺ともしらず
nobe tomo shirazu

旅寝して
tabine shite

うまき都の
umaki miyako no

夢をくはれき
yume wo kuwareki

鹿都部真顔
Shikatsube no Magao

*Not knowing it was a field
where baku sport, I slept
my traveller's sleep—and had
my sweet dream of Miyako
gobbled up!*

Kyōka Saizōshū Book 7, Travel. In the world of *kyōka* (literally, "crazy poems": witty poems in the tanka form) in the 1780s, Shikatsube no Magao was a figure second in importance only to Yomono Akara. He started out as owner of a *shiruko* (sweet bean-soup) store in Edo's Sukiyabashi district, but later became a professional teacher of *kyōka* and had many followers.

The poem's title is "Travel Dream." The subject is a rare one: the imaginary animal called *baku*, which is said to be fond of eating dreams. Were it a tanka, the traveller's dream would have to express longing for Miyako, the capital. The *kyōka*, however, laughs that off. Instead, the dreamer, unaware of the baku's presence, has his sweet dream of Miyako gobbled up before he can enjoy it.

つぶらなる
Tsubura naru
汝が眼吻はなん
na ga me suwanan
露の秋
Tsuyu no aki
飯田蛇笏
Iida Dakotsu

Your full, round
eyes I'll sip—
Dew of autumn

From *Sanroshū* (Mountain Hut, 1932). Written in 1914, at age 29. In the same year, Dakotsu wrote this elegant haiku, which deeply impressed Akutagawa Ryūnosuke: Mortally ill, / her fingernails so beautiful / on the brazier (*Shibyō ete tsume utsukushiki hioke kana*). But he also wrote poems of artless purity, like the one above.

The character 吻 means "lip", not "sip". *Suwanan* should properly be *suinan*. So, strictly speaking, there are two mistakes. However, if they were corrected to *suinan* 吸ひなん, the poem would be ruined. Conjuring up a kiss, the poet speaks only of eyes. A simple poem, but a masterful one.

白妙の
Shirotae no

袖のわかれに
sode no wakare ni

露おちて
tsuyu ochite

身にしむ色の
mi ni shimu iro no

秋風ぞふく
akikaze zo fuku

藤原定家
Fujiwara no Teika

On foam-white sleeves at parting,
  dew drops fall,
    color of the weeping heart
    and of the wind,
      whose autumn sting dyes all

This poem begins Book 15, the fifth and last section of love poems in the *Shinkokinshū*. One of the greatest poems by the medieval poet (and man) who stands supreme in the tone known as "ethereal charm," it expresses a woman's feelings as she grieves over parting from her lover at dawn.

Tsuyu, "dew" is the dawn dew, but also means the woman's tears, falling on her sleeves. *Aki*, "autumn", includes the homonymous *aki*, "to tire of", and hints at the woman's abandonment. The phrase *mi ni shimu iro*, "color that stings the heart", is one of consummate skill, but also an alchemic reworking of an old poem: "It blew this way / and stung my heart / O autumn wind, / once I thought / you had no color!" (*Fuki kureba mi ni mo shimikeru akikaze wo iro naki mono to omoi-keru kana*)

未婚の吾の
Mikon no ware no

夫のにあらずや
tsuma no ni arazu ya

海に向き
Umi ni muki

白き墓碑ありて
shiroki bohi arite

薄日あたれる
usubi atareru

富小路禎子
Tominokōji Yoshiko

*This must be for
the husband I never wed
A white grave marker
faces the sea,
lit up by the fading sun*

From *Hakugyō* (White Dawn, 1970). A tanka poet of the war generation, and a student of Uematsu Hisaki. Another of her poems from this period is: "When autumn comes / to a room / where a woman lives alone / mirrors shine out / from everything there" (*Onna hitori sumu heya no uchi ni aki kureba nabete no naka ni kagami tachikuru*).

To a strong-willed woman of middle-age who has never married comes a vision to disturb her peace of mind. She writes of it with deep yet unsentimental pathos: this sudden possession by the irrational feeling that a grave marker facing the sea must be that of her own husband, though she never married.

神無月
Kaminazuki

降りみ降らずみ
furimi furazumi

定めなき
sadamenaki

時雨ぞ冬の
shigure zo fuyu no

はじめなりける
hajime narikeru

よみ人しらず
Yomibito shirazu

In the godless month
the rains come and go,
come and go.
Their fierce ephemeral bursts
are winter's beginning.

Anonymous

Gosenshū, Book 8, Winter. *Kaminazuki* was the tenth month in the lunar calendar. By modern reckoning, it begins in mid-November.

Shigure are the brief but heavy rains of late autumn through winter. In the *Man'yōshū* they were treated as autumnal, but in the *Kokinshū*, they were placed among the first winter poems, and from then on became an early winter topic. Perhaps there was a subtle change in the sense of season after the capital's move from Nara to Kyoto. This poem of the late 10th century is like the formal assertion of a popular notion that began about this time.

沖の石の
Oki no ishi no

ひそかに産みし
hisoka ni umishi

海鼠かな
namako kana

野村喜舟
Nomura Kishū

The offshore rock
secretly gave birth—
to a sea cucumber

From *Koishikawa*, 1952. Kishū, a modern haiku poet born in 1886 in Kanazawa, Ishikawa Prefecture, moved to Tokyo as a child. A life-long disciple of Matsune Tōyōjō, he succeeded him as editor of the haiku magazine *Shibugaki*.

Perhaps because of its strange shape, the sea cucumber since olden times has often been the subject of humorous haiku. This one stands apart because it brings to mind a love poem by Nijō-in no Sanuki from the medieval collection *Ogura Hyakunin Isshu*: "My sleeve / an offshore rock / unseen at low tide, / no one knows how / it is never dry" (*Waga sode wa shiohi ni mienu oki no ishi no hito koso shirane kawaku ma mo nashi*). In this tanka, the offshore rock is just like a woman damp with tears of unrequited love.

It's amusing to imagine that the offshore rock identified with the weeping woman is also the one that secretly gave birth to a sea cucumber.

豊年のしるしは
Toyotoshi no shirushi wa

尺に満ちて降る雪
shaku ni michite furu yuki

中古雑唱集
Chūko Zasshōshū

Sign of an abundant year:
A full foot's fall of snow

A brief song recorded in the secret teachings of the Ayanokōji family, hereditary performers of traditional vocal music since the Heian period. It was one of the lyrics sung during the Imperial Gosechi festival and at court banquets.

Even with today's urbanized life, people sometimes rejoice at a big snowfall, but the celebratory tone of poems like this has almost died out. A year of much snow is not necessarily a plentiful year, but it used to be that the perception of seasonal phenomena was inseparable from an intense interest in forecasting whether the harvest would be good or bad. One can't just lightly say that people look on the landscape now with the same eyes that they did of old.

志賀の浦や
Shiga no ura ya

遠ざかりゆく
Tōzakari yuku

波間より
namima yori

凍りていづる
kōrite izuru

有明けの月
ariake no tsuki

藤原家隆
Fujiwara no Ietaka

Shiga Bay—
  The waves move off
    into the distance
      and from them, frozen,
        climbs the dawn moon

Shinkokinshū, Book 6, Winter. Written on the topic "Winter Moon on the Lake" for a poem competition at the house of Minister of the Left Fujiwara Yoshitsune.

Shiga Bay is one of the bays of Lake Biwa. The poem describes the moon rising over the lake in the depths of winter at early dawn, when the air is coldest. The water near the shore freezes first, so the waves "move off into the distance" from the beach. From those distant waves, the moon rises very late at night, almost at dawn, thin and frozen. A union of clarity, desolation, and strength.

This poem intentionally echoes the winter *Goshūishū* poem: "Now late at night / is the shore frozen? / Far off / into the distance / move the waves of Shiga Bay" (*Sayo fukuru mama ni nagisa ya kōruramu Tozakariyuku Shiga no uranami*).

咳の子の
Seki no ko no

なぞなぞあそび
nazonazo asobi

きりもなや
kiri mo naya

中村汀女
Nakamura Teijo

My coughing child's
riddle games
know no end

From *Teijo Kushū*, 1944. There are many female haiku poets, but Teijo must be the best example of one who was able to harmonize in the happiest way the demands of family life and poetry. The fact that many of her best poems were about her own children was related to this.

A sick child in bed begs his mother to play with him and forgets himself in telling riddles one after another. He goes on and on even while coughing.

元日や
Ganjitsu ya

暗き空より
Kuraki sora yori

風が吹く
kaze ga fuku

青木月斗
Aoki Getto

New Year's Day—
From a dark sky
wind blows

From *Getto-ō Kushū*, 1950. Born in Osaka, this haiku poet died in 1949, at 69. His family ran a pharmaceutical business. Among Masaoka Shiki's followers in western Japan, he was so highly valued that Shiki sent him this poem: "Oh you, the magistrate / of haikai in the west— / moonlit autumn" (*Haikai no nishi no bugyō ya Tsuki no aki*).

Good New Year's poems are always in short supply. This is an unusual one, fresh and yet mysterious. The wind blowing from a dark sky is not a phenomenon limited to New Year's Day, of course, but Getto has seized it and used it in such a vivid way that I have the feeling of witnessing one of those moments when life and poetry intersect.

さねさし
Sanesashi

相模の小野に
Sagamu no ono ni

燃ゆる火の
moyuru hi no

火中に立ちて
honaka ni tachite

問ひし君はも
toishi kimi wa mo

古事記歌謡
Kojiki Kayō

*In the little field
of Sagamu, the fires
burned, the fires—and
you stood there among them
and said you loved me*

Kojiki song

When the god of Sagamu Sea tried to keep Yamato Takeru from crossing and made the sea so rough that Yamato Takeru's ship was almost wrecked, his consort Ototachibana jumped into the sea and stilled the waves. This poem is given in the *Kojiki* as the farewell poem she recited in her last moments.

Sanesashi is a pillow word for Sagamu. The meaning of the poem in the *Kojiki* context is: "When we met the enemy's fires in Sagamu's fields, even in the midst of the flames you said you loved me." But if read apart from the legend of Yamato Takeru, this is a farmer's love song, and the meaning is: "In the early spring, the fields were being burned and at the fires' height, it was you who said, 'Please marry me.'", for the original meaning of *toishi* is from *tsumadoi*, to propose marriage.

朝影に
Asakage ni

わが身はなりぬ
waga mi wa narinu

玉かぎる
Tamakagiru

ほのかに見えて
honoka ni miete

去にし子ゆえに
inishi ko yue ni

柿本人麻呂歌集
"Kakinomoto no
Hitomaro Kashū"

*My body's turned to
a morning shadow
because of a girl I saw,
faint as jewel light,
then saw no more*
　　　　　　"The Hitomaro Collection"

Man'yōshū, Book 9. "The Hitomaro Collection"
is an old tanka collection which was in existence at
the time the *Man'yōshū* itself was compiled.
Hitomaro himself may not have authored all of its
poems, but many are excellent and repay repeated
readings, including this love poem.

Asakage, morning shadow, is the weak shadow
things cast at daybreak. *Tamakagiru*, jewel light, is
a *makurakotoba* (pillow word) used to modify *hono-
ka*, faint, perhaps because a jewel gives off a faint
light.

The poem is about wasting away from love but it
has a captivating beauty.

幼馴染みに離れたをりは

Osananajimi ni hanareta ori wa

沖の櫓櫂が折れたよな

oki no rokai ga oreta yo na

山家鳥虫歌

Sanka Chōchūka

Being far from my childhood friend
is like having my oar break on the high sea

"Poems of Mountain Huts, Birds and Bugs"

A mid-Edo period collection of songs published in **1772.** The contents, which consist mainly of lyrics from all over Japan for dances of the summer Festival of the Dead, are thought to date from the early Edo period and after. They are a mine of information about the relationship between folk song and popular song.

This song is from the province of Iga (part of modern Mie Prefecture) and describes how forlorn it is to be parted from a childhood friend. Read by itself, it would seem to be about male friendship, but probably, like most folk songs, it is about male-female love.

Hanareta, "far from", is a flexible word, capable of suggesting many meanings.

春みじかし
Haru mijikashi

何に不滅の
nan ni fumetsu no

命ぞと
inochi zo to

ちからある乳を
chikara aru chi wo

手にさぐらせぬ
te ni sagurasenu

与謝野晶子
Yosano Akiko

'Spring is short—
What has eternal life?'
I thought, and
let his hands seek out
my strong breasts

An extremely famous poem from *Midaregami* (Tangled Hair, 1901). The idea that youth is short and nothing lives forever is an ancient one but no tanka poet has ever expressed it as boldly as this poem in its last two lines. I think the daring was strictly in the realm of fantasy, however, product of the extravagant imagination of a young girl brought up in a merchant family (owners of the Surugaya confectionery in Sakai) who found her escape in the world of medieval romances.

Perhaps because she was stung by the ridicule of the critics, Akiko later rewrote the last line as *te ni saguru ware*, "I seek out", so that the speaker herself touches her own breasts, but I prefer the original.

雪はげし
Yuki hageshi

抱かれて息の
Dakarete iki no

つまりしこと
tsumarishi koto

橋本多佳子
Hashimoto Takako

Fierce snow
Once, embraced,
my breath stopped

From *Kōshi* (Red Thread, 1951). Takako studied haiku with Sugita Hisajo and latter joined Yamaguchi Seishi's haiku group. She expressed the eruptions and flickerings of female emotion with a fresh and sure touch. She is one of the best modern women writers in terms of her discipline as a poet and range of expression.

Widowed in her late thirties, Takako wrote many moving poems in memory of her husband. This is one of the best known. Staring at the furiously falling snow, she calls up from within that sight a memory of equal intensity.

わたつ海の
Watatsumi no

沖に火もゆる
oki ni hi moyuru

火の国に
Hi no kuni ni

我あり誰そや
ware ari Ta so ya

思はれ人は
omowarebito wa

柳原白蓮
Yanagihara Byakuren

The high seas
blaze with flame
I live in
a land on fire

Who is my true love?

From *Maboroshi no Hana* (Phantom Flower, 1919). Byakuren was born in Tokyo and died in 1967 at age 81. Her father was a count. After her first marriage failed, she married Itō Denemon, a coal magnate of northern Kyushu, but that marriage did not work out either. She left the Itō family, married the social activist Miyazaki Ryūsuke and after the war participated in the peace movement. Her tanka teacher was Sasaki Nobutsuna.

The second line, *oki ni hi moyuru*, refers to phosphorescent light, and is an introductory phrase for "a land on fire", another name for the Tsukushi area of Kyushu.

The poem dates from the painful days of her loveless marriage with a millionaire. Ardent love spills out of the defiant question with which the poem ends.

みずうみの
Mizu-umi no

氷は解けて
kōri wa tokete

なほ寒し
nao samushi

三日月の影
Mikazuki no kage

波にうつろふ
nami ni utsurou

島木赤彦
Shimagi Akahiko

The ice on the lake
is melting but
it's still cold
The crescent moon's light
flickers over the waves

From *Taikyoshū* (The Great Void, 1924), "On the Banks of Lake Suwa."

Akahiko's house was (and still remains) on a piece of land looking down diagonally on Lake Suwa. This is one of the very best of the many excellent poems Akahiko left about the lake, which he loved.

The ice that has completely covered the lake has begun to melt but it is still bitterly cold. The slender thread-like form of the crescent moon casts a shimmering reflection on the waves. It gives off a light that can hardly be called light—quiet, and of immeasurable depth.

谷風に
Tanikaze ni

解くる氷の
tokuru kōri no

ひまごとに
himagoto ni

うち出づる波や
uchi-izuru nami ya

春の初花
haru no hatsuhana

源当純
Minamoto no Masazumi

Out of the cracks in
the ice melted by
the valley breeze,
spout waves—
spring's first flowers

Kokinshū, Book 1, Spring. A poet who lived in the early 10th century, when the *Kokinshū* was completed. Son of Minister of the Right Minamoto no Yoshiari, he was a Minor Counselor, Junior Fifth Rank Upper Grade.

The poem is about early spring. The first two lines allude to the old Chinese calendrical expression *tōfū kaihyō*, "eastern breezes melt the ice". White waves dance up out of every break in the ice, which has begun to melt in the spring breezes. In early spring, there are still no flowers, but are not these waves, says the poet, the real first flowers? A spirited, happy poem.

春寒し
Haru samushi

水田の上の
Mizuta no ue no

根なし雲
nenashigumo

河東碧梧桐
Kawahigashi Hekigotō

Spring chill
Above rice paddies
rootless clouds

From *Shinhaiku* (New Haiku, 1898).

Hekigotō was born in 1873 and died in 1937. Like Takahama Kyoshi, he was a leading figure in the haiku reform that centered around Masaoka Shiki, the older friend of both. All three poets hailed from Matsuyama City in Shikoku.

After Shiki's death, Hekigotō took a solitary path and pioneered the New Tendency haiku. His path diverged radically from that of Kyoshi, whose advocacy of a more orthodox style called Flowers and Birds brought him great success.

The poem above is an early one; Shiki praised it highly. It is not especially original in scene or mood, but the transparency of the 'rootless clouds' is redolent of the chilliness of spring.

Looking backwards, this poem almost seems to hint at the trajectory of its author's life.

ただ吟じて臥すべし梅花の月
Tada ginjite fusubeshi baika no tsuki

仏となり天に生ずれど
Hotoke to nari ten ni shōzuredo

すべて是れ虚
subete kore kyo

閑吟集
Kanginshū

Just sing to the plum blossoms
under the moon,
then go to bed
So what if you become a Buddha
and go to heaven, —— in the end
it's all the same void

A Muromachi period folk song. The original is in *kanbun*, that is, classical Chinese read as if it were Japanese. From olden days, lines from classical Chinese poems were very popular as lyrics for Japanese folk songs. The Muromachi period was the height of the Five Mountains literature of Zen monasteries, which was in *kanbun*, and so lines like these found their way even into a collection of contemporary folk-songs like the *Kanginshū*.

The poet recommends we just enjoy the flowers, sing poems to them, then go to sleep. Becoming a Buddha and being born again in heaven is just as empty as the things of this world.

The delight of this poem comes from the way it turns coventional values on their head in Zen style, praising nothingness and a mad devotion to beauty.

雪ながら
Yuki nagara

山本かすむ
yamamoto kasumu

夕べかな
yūbe kana

宗祇
Sōgi

Though snow remains,
haze hides the mountain foot
this twilit evening

行く水遠く
Yuku mizu tōku

梅匂ふ里
ume niou sato

肖柏
Shōhaku

Water flows far off
to a village fragrant with plum

川風に
Kawakaze ni

ひとむら柳
hitomura yanagi

春見えて
haru miete

宗長
Sōchō

River breezes
on a group of willows,
spring appearing

The opening of the famous 100–stanza *renga* sequence *Minase Sangin* (Three Poets at Minase). Sōgi was the foremost renga poet of the middle Muromachi period; the other two were his leading disciples. This renga was an offering to the Minase shrine of Retired Emperor Gotoba-in, who had been deeply involved with both waka and renga.

The first link alludes to Gotoba-in's tanka, "When I look far off, / haze hides the mountain foot along Minase River / Why did I think that / twilight was best in autumn ?". (*Miwataseba yamamoto kasumu Minasegawa Yūbe wa aki to nani omoiken*). While there is still snow on the mountain peak, spring mists obscure the foot. A thawed stream flows far off, to a village already scented with plum blossoms. And in the green of the willow trees that sway in the river breeze, spring is visible.

冬眠より
Tōmin yori

醒めし蛙が
sameshi kaeru ga

残雪の
zansetsu no

うへにのぼりて
ue ni noborite

体を平ぶ
karada wo hirabu

斎藤茂吉
Saitō Mokichi

Woken from winter sleep,
the frogs ascend
the last thin layer of snow
and spread
their bodies flat

From *Shirokiyama* (White Mountains, 1949). Mokichi was a tanka poet who was born in Yamagata Prefecture in 1882 and died in 1953. He was evacuated from Tokyo to his original home in the closing days of World War II, but instead of returning to Tokyo at the war's end, he stayed on, moving in early spring of the next year to the Ōishida region near the Mogami River. There he lived alone for over a year.

This poem dates from early spring of 1947, when Mokichi was in the habit of taking his lunch and walking about near the Mogami River. The precision of the last line, "spread their bodies flat", pulls the whole poem together and at the same time opens it up. A truly skillful poem.

ねがはくは
Negawaku wa

花のもとにて
hana no moto ni te

春死なむ
haru shinamu

その如月の
Sono kisaragi no

望月のころ
mochizuki no koro

西行法師
Saigyō Hōshi

In spring let me die,
  beneath the cherry trees,
    as the second month moon rounds full

Shinkokinshū, Miscellaneous Poems. This is one of Saigyō's most famous poems, but during the process of compilation it was removed from the *Shinkokinshū* and remained only in a variant edition.

Kisaragi no mochizuki no koro means the full moon of the 15th day of the second lunar month, which corresponds to late March in the solar calendar. This would be the peak of the cherry blossoms that Saigyō loved so much, as well as the day of the Buddha's death and entrance into nirvana. It was natural for Saigyō, who was a Buddhist monk, to hope to die on that day, but surprisingly enough, he actually did die on the 16th day of the second lunar month, 1190.

廻る杖は空を飛びて
Meguru tsue wa sora wo tobite

初月かと疑ふ
mikazuki ka to utagau

奔る毬は地を転びて
Hashiru mari wa chi wo marobite

流星に似る
ryūsei ni niru

嵯峨天皇
Saga Tennō

*The curved stick might be
a crescent moon flying across the sky
The rushing ball resembles
a comet tumbling to earth*

Keikokushū, Book 11. From a poem in Chinese entitled "Watching *dakyū* in early spring." In the early Heian period envoys from the Chinese state of Bo Hai, with which Japan then had thriving relations, used the fragrant spring gardens of the Imperial palace to show their hosts *dakyū*, a ball game rather like polo, played on horseback to the accompaniment of music. This unusual poem described it.

The comparison of the stick that drives the ball to a crescent moon came from the stick's curved shape. Emperor Saga was an enthusiastic advocate of continental culture and good friends with Kūkai (Kōbō Daishi). Famed as well for his calligraphy, he is considered, with Kūkai and Tachibana no Hayanari, to be one of the three great masters of that art.

わが肩に
Waga kata ni

春の世界の
haru no sekai no

もの一つ
mono hitotsu

くづれ来しやと
kuzure koshi ya to

御手を思ひし
mite wo omoishi

与謝野晶子
Yosano Akiko

I thought it perhaps
a fragment, broken loose
from the world of spring—
your hand upon
my shoulder

From *Yume no Hana* (Dream Flowers, 1906). Is this a memory of the early days of acquaintance with her husband, Yosano Hiroshi? The abstract phrase *haru no sekai no mono hitotsu* (a fragment... from the world of spring) here, paradoxically, gives birth to the most concrete of impressions. There would have been days when the hand of the man she loved, placed casually on her shoulder, brought fresh and joyous surprise.

Akiko had been married five years when she wrote this poem. Some of her poems from this time are about suffering greatly from jealousy: "Fearful heart / awaked from love, / what do you see? / Is there no prison / to take my eyes?" (*Osoroshiki koizamegokoro nani wo miru Waga me toraemu hitoya wa naki ya*) And yet she loved Hiroshi to the end of her life, and never stopped celebrating him.

雀子の
Suzumeko no

もの喰夢か
mono kuu yume ka

夜のこゑ
Yoru no koe

松岡青蘿
Matsuoka Seira

Is it the sparrow's child,
dreaming of food?
A voice in the night

From *Seira Hokkushū*. He represented the Himeji domain in Edo, but a fondness for gambling made him lose his position. He became a *rōnin* (masterless samurai), and then a monk. As he wandered Japan, he composed haikai and became one of its foremost masters during the haikai revival of the late eighteenth century.

Sparrow chicks leave the nest in late spring or early summer. One night the poet happens to hear a chick cry out in the dark. It must have sounded a little sleepy, different from its shrill clamor at a parental feeding during the day.

There is a similar poem by Bashō: "Cries echo back and forth / between the sparrows' children / and the mouse's nest" (*Suzumeko to koe nakikawasu nezumi no su*).

まだ知らぬ
Mada shiranu

清さなりけり
kiyosa narikeri

燈台の
Tōdai no

曲れる段を
magareru dan wo

我がのぼる音
waga noboru oto

与謝野　寛（鉄幹）
Yosano Hiroshi (Tekkan)

It was a purity
I had not known:
The sound as I climbed
the winding
lighthouse stairs

Yosano Hiroshi died March 26, 1935, age 62. This tanka was written on March 3, when, in spite of a cold, he visited Kannonzaki, site of the first Western-style lighthouse in Japan. This is the last poem of the free spirit who led the tanka reform of the Meiji period.

Its crystalline quality is one with another poem, written in his prime: "Why do I think of myself / as a speck of dust / in the vast sky? / Tears flow down / my face" (*Ōzora no chiri to wa ikaga omoubeki Atsuki namida no nagaruru mono wo*). Hiroshi expressed passionate emotion with naked clarity.

ゆく春や
Yuku haru ya

蓬が中の
Yomogi ga naka no

人の骨
hito no hone

榎本星布
Enomoto Seifu

Spring is passing by—
Among the lush yomogi,
human bones

From *Seifu-ni Kushū* (Haiku by the Nun Seifu). A woman poet active in the haikai revival of the late eighteenth century. Her teacher was Kaya Shirao.

Tōyūki (Journey to the East), a travel account by Seifu's contemporary, the doctor and man of letters Tachibana Nankei, records in wrenching detail the great famine of the early 1780s in northern Japan. This poem may also be a witness to that time.

In a wild field at the end of spring, clumps of *yomogi* (mugwort) grow thickly, full of life. Among them are scattered the bones of people who starved to death in the freezing winter. How many haiku poets, of either sex, could write about such a topic?

うちしめり
Uchishimeri

あやめぞかをる
ayame zo kaoru

ほととぎす
Hototogisu

鳴くや五月の
naku ya Satsuki no

雨の夕暮
ame no yūgure

藤原良経
Fujiwara no Yoshitsune

Fifth-month rain
at evening:
The fragrance of
wet irises,
a cuckoo's call

Shinkokinshū, Book 3, Summer. Born into the prestigious Fujiwara family, this poet of the early Kamakura period rose to become Imperial Regent.

The poem alludes to one of the best known love poems in the *Kokinshū*, an anonymous one in Book 11: "A cuckoo calls/as Fifth-month iris blooms, / while I am dark, / blinded / with unknown love" (*Hototogisu naku ya Satsuki no ayamegusa ayame mo shiranu koi mo suru kana*). Yoshitsune took over the cuckoo, the irises, and the month as is, but changed the subject from love to the summer season: on the ground, damp irises release their fragrance, while in the sky a cuckoo passing by cries out from time to time.

Yoshitsune's skill is evident from the fact that he was able to evoke quite a different effect from the earlier poem even while using very similar words.

雲碧落に消えて天の膚解く
Kumo hekiraku ni kiete ten no hadae toku

風清漪を動かして水の面皺めり
Kaze sei-i wo ugokashite mizu no omote shiwameri

都良香
Miyako no Yoshika

Clouds vanish into the azure sky:
heaven's skin melts

Winds run over the rippling waves:
the water's face wrinkles

Wakan Rōeishū, Book 2, Fine Weather.
Miyako no Yoshika was a scholar and poet
of Chinese in the early Heian period. As
the leading scholar and literary figure of
the time, he drafted many imperial procla-
mations and documents.

The poem describes an interval of clear
weather during early summer rains. The
first two lines liken the clouds to the skin
of the sky; the last two compare the water
to a face. A very simple poem, but when
set to music it must have been quite lovely.

子は裸
Ko wa hadaka

Naked child,

父はててれで
chichi wa teterede

father in a loin-cloth—

早苗舟
sanaebune

the seedling boat

利牛
Rigyū

岸のいばらの
Kishi no ibara no

On the bank, wild roses

真白に咲く
masshiro ni saku

bloom, pure white

野坡
Yaba

雨あがり
Ame-agari

Rain passed,

数珠懸鳩の
zuzukakebato no

the ring-doves

鳴出して
nakidashite

sing on

孤屋
Ko-oku

The first three links of "One Hundred Stanzas", a sequence in *A Sack of Charcoal*, one of the haikai collections of Bashō's later years,

Sanaebune, "seedling boat", is a small boat piled with rice seedlings. The father and son push it along through the wet rice paddy as they transplant the seedlings. *Zuzukakebato*, "ring-dove", is a small dove with a black, necklace-shaped crest at the nape of the neck. *Sanaebune* and *ibara no hana*, "wild roses", are both summer season words, and evoke the freshness of rice transplanting time.

The style of Bashō and his disciples at this time was *karumi*, lightness.

青空より
Aozora yori

破片あつめて
hahen atsumete

きしごとき
kishi gotoki

愛語を言えり
aigo wo ieri

われに抱かれて
Ware ni dakarete

寺山修司
Terayama Shūji

Your loving words
when I embraced you
were like fragments
you had gathered for me
from the azure sky

From *Sora ni wa Hon* (Books in the Sky, 1958). Born 1936 in Aomori Prefecture, this tanka poet and leader of his own theatrical troupe died in 1983. He was an avant-garde artist with great talent as a lyric poet. Although he died young, I feel sure that young peple will be reciting his poems of youthful love for years to come.

Aigo, "loving words", was originally a Buddhist term. Here it is used to mean the affectionate murmurs of a young and innocent girl.

The first three (in translation, the last three) lines, with their delicacy, convey the fresh sensation of life, of youth itself.

橋の下なるめめ雑魚だにも
Hashi no shita naru meme jako danimo

独りは寝じと上り下る
hitori wa neji to nobori kudaru

閑吟集
Kanginshū

Even the little fish that live
  beneath the bridges
hate to sleep alone;
  up the river they go, then down

The *Kanginshū* is a Muromachi period collection of 311 folk songs. Since the songs were popular ones, many of them are about love, and of these many concern the loneliness of sleeping alone. In this, they are like the classical waka anthologies compiled by the court. The theme of the loneliness of sleeping alone runs like a river through the history of Japanese love poetry.

Meme jako are small fish like killifish. The poet means: "Even little fish like them, not liking to sleep alone, go up and down the river in schools, while I must sleep miserable and alone." Many other poems in the *Kanginshū* express the same idea.

みじか夜や
Mijikayo ya

毛むしの上に
Kemushi no ue ni

露の玉
tsuyu no tama

与謝蕪村
Yosa Buson

Brief night !
Atop the caterpillar,
a dewdrop

From *Buson Kushū*. *Mijikayo*, "brief night", is a season word for summer: just as one thinks it's really late, the day dawns. On the tip of a caterpillar's downy hair, faintly visible, a drop of dew.

Caterpillars are not the most popular of insects. How like Buson to blithely place the dawn dew on one's back, thus creating with a flick of the brush a vision of refreshing coolness. Had he said *ue no* instead of *ue ni*, the weight would have fallen on the last line, *tsuyu no tama*, emphasizing the dewdrop's concrete physicality and giving rise to a different effect. A modern haiku poet might in fact be more likely to choose the latter route.

ゆふだちの
Yūdachi no

雲飛びわくる
kumo tobiwakuru

白鷺の
shirasagi no

つばさにかけて
tsubasa ni kakete

晴るる日の影
haruru hi no kage

花園院
Hanazono-in

Snowy herons
fly through clouds
left by evening showers
On their wings
clear sunlight shines

Fūgashū, Summer. Hanazono was the 95th emperor. He lived in a chaotic time, when the Imperial house had split into two opposing lines and the new Yoshino court had been established, but he loved learning, was well-versed in the teachings of Buddhism and Confucianism and studied Zen Buddhism deeply. His poetry teacher was Kyōgoku Tamekane, the leading poet of the time, and his poems are thoroughly thought out.

The summer rainstorm has passed over, but clouds are still hanging low. The snowy herons fly through them as though pushing their way through, the sun lighting up their wings. Washed by the rain, the world shines anew.

夜の向日葵
Yo no himawari

踊り果てたる
odori hatetaru

ごとく立つ
gotoku tatsu

宮津昭彦
Miyatsu Akihiko

Evening sunflowers
linger,
like danced-out dancers

From *Sekiun* (Cumulus Clouds, 1961). A haiku poet, born 1929 in Yokohama. From his mid-teens Miyatsu was a close disciple of the haiku poet and critic Ōno Rinka, then a teacher of economic history at the commercial high-school Miyatsu attended. In his introduction to *Sekiun*, Rinka wrote: "I loved the sharpness of his sensibility, and on his once or twice monthly visits, I used to welcome him almost as I would have welcomed a lover, devouring the notebook in which he wrote his poems."

The precision of the personified simile makes this poem memorable.

往事眇茫として
Ōji byōbō to shite

都て夢に似たり
subete yume ni nitari

旧遊零落して
Kyūyū reiraku shite

半ば泉に帰す
nakaba sen ni kisu

白居易（白楽天）
Po Chü-i

The past is infinitely far,
  all, all seems a dream
The old friends have withered like leaves,
  half of them returned to the other world

Wakan Rōeishū, Book 2, "Remembrance". No foreign poet, classical or modern, has left as much of a mark on the world of traditional Japanese poetry and music as the Chinese poet Po Chü-i, known as Haku Kyo-i or Haku Raku-ten in Japanese.

This is one stanza from a longer poem about unexpectedly meeting an old poet friend after many years. For the middle-aged poet, the joy of meeting again imperceptibly blended into a lament for life's passing. Such emotions never change.

蛸壺や
Takotsubo ya

はかなき夢を
Hakanaki yume wo

夏の月
Natsu no tsuki

松尾芭蕉
Matsuo Bashō

Octopus pots!
Fleeting dreams,
a summer moon . . .

On his trip of 1688 to western Japan, Bashō visited Suma and Akashi. This haiku appears in his travel journal from that time, *Oi no Kobumi*.

Takotsubo, "octopus pots": unpainted ceramic pots which used the propensity of octopuses for hiding in holes as a way to trap them. The fishermen lowered the pots to the bottom of the sea during the day, then pulled them up before dawn.

On brief summer nights, the moon lights up the sea. In the darkness of a pot on the sea floor, a living creature swirls about, dreaming fleeting dreams of a life brief as the night. On first reading, the poem has a deep feeling of pathos, but at its core lies *okashi*, a kind of humorous detachment toward the absurdity of life that is often found in haikai.

遺児の手の
Iji no te no

かくもやはらか
kakumo yawaraka

秋の風
Aki no kaze

飯田蛇笏
Iida Dakotsu

An orphan's hand—
how can it be this soft?
The autumn wind

From *Sekkyō* (Snow Straits, 1951). Dakotsu, a leading haiku poet in the Taishō and Shōwa periods, had five sons. Three fought in World War II, and of them two were killed. His eldest son Sōichirō (haiku pen name Hōsei) met his death in Leyte at the end of 1944, leaving behind a daughter who had been born after he was called up. The notice of his death did not come to his family until three years later.

Dakotsu also wrote: "This frosty night / I hold a soldier's child by the hearth / What can I do?" (*Hei no ko wo ro ni daku shimoya Ika ni sen*) and "I see his form / in the child / Days and nights of dew" (*Omokage wo ko ni miru Tsuyu no nichiya kana*). The infinitely soft hand of a child who never knew a father. The autumn wind.

山里は
Yamazato wa

松の声のみ
matsu no koe nomi

ききなれて
kikinarete

風ふかぬ日は
kaze fukanu hi wa

寂しかりけり
sabishikarikeri

太田垣蓮月
Ōtagaki Rengetsu

In the mountain village
my ears know only
the voice of the pines—
windless days
are lonely

From *Ama no Karumo*. A tanka poet, Rengetsu was born in Kyoto in 1791 and died 1875, aged 84. Her four children all died young and after she was widowed at thirty, she became a Buddhist nun. As a means of livelihood, she made pottery, a craft she had taught herself, The artistry of her work, as well as her many talents and her beauty, brought her great renown. She disliked visitors drawn only by vulgar curiosity, however. To find peace and quiet, she moved about from place to place in the Kyoto area, living simply. The elegance of her unadorned style and the deep peace of her poems leave a lasting impression.

夕星は
Yūzutsu wa

かがやく朝が八方に
kagayaku asa ga happō ni

散らしたものを
chirashita mono wo

みな
mina

もとへ
moto e

連れかへす
tsurekaesu

サッポー
Sappho

呉茂一訳
(translated by Kure Shigeichi)

The evening star
brings home
to their beginning
all that shining morning scattered
to the eight directions.

One of the few extant lyrics by the famous woman poet of Greece, born on the island of Lesbos in the seventh century before Christ. After the lines above she wrote, "It brings back the sheep, / brings back the goat, / brings home the child to her mother's hand." This poem has been known in Japan since the Meiji period, thanks to the translation of Ueda Bin in 1896.

The quiet glow of the stars begins to light up the sky at dusk. The image of the evening star gathering in and tying together what "morning scattered to the eight directions" is beautiful. This was the vision of one woman, a poet long ago in a country far away, but it still lives now.

うたたねに
Utatane ni

恋しき人を
koishiki hito wo

見てしより
miteshi yori

夢てふものは
yume chō mono wa

たのみそめてき
tanomi someteki

小野小町
Ono no Komachi

Briefly I slept
and saw
the one I love
Now I place my faith
in this thing called dreams

Kokinshū, Book 12, Love. Komachi is considered one of the Six Poetic Immortals and an example of the misfortunes that beauty can bring, but in fact little is known of her life. The only records we have are her poignant and beautiful poems.

Book 12 of the *Kokinshū* begins with three poems by Komachi, of which this is one. All three are about brief dreams; doubtless the compilers planned this consciously.

Komachi alludes to the then-popular belief that dreaming of the person you loved meant that he or she desired you. The poem's undercurrent is a lament that although she once met her lover in a dream, now he never comes, not even in dreams.

後影を
Ushirokage wo

　見んとすれば
　min to sureba

　　霧がなう
　　kiri ga nō

　　　朝霧が
　　　asagiri ga

　　　　閑吟集
　　　　Kanginshū

I strained to see
his retreating figure—
but the mists,
the morning mists!

A popular song of the Muromachi period. From ancient through medieval times the basic form of love affairs and marriages was matrilocal. The man visited at night and left with the rooster's crow. Even after the shift to patrilocal marriage where the woman came to live with the man, there was no change for courtesans and others like them.

"Together but one night / and feeling sad to part / I came out to look for you / But your boat in the offing / was so quick and the mist so thick!" (*Hitoyo nareta ga nagori oshisa ni idete mitareba okinaka ni fune no hayasa yo kiri no fukasa yo*) (*Kanginshū*)—this poem is of course by "a woman of the harbor". Such longings are expressed even more intensely in the first poem above. A sigh itself becomes a poem . . .

歯が抜てから
Ha ga nukete kara

顔の静さ
kao no shizukesa

武玉川
Mutamagawa

After the teeth go,
how quiet is the face

The mid-18th century *Mutamagawa* is an 18-volume compendium of the best stanzas from innumerable contemporary *renku* linked-verse sequences, each anonymous stanza presented as an independent poem. Many of its brief pieces show a keen insight into life, reaffirming how interesting the poetry of ordinary people can be.

With age, the teeth loosen and fall out. One by one they go, taking self-confidence and audacity with them. It is clever to use the sketch of a toothless face to capture old age, but the scaffolding is the pithy and precise use of words.

留守と言え
Rusu to ie

ここには誰も居らぬと言え
Koko ni wa dare mo oranu to ie

五億年経ったら帰って来る
Go-oku nen tattara kaette kuru

高橋新吉
Takahashi Shinkichi

Say I'm out
Say no one's here
In five hundred million years
I'll come home

From *Takahashi Shinkichi no Shinshū*, 1949. Born in Ehime Prefecture, this modern poet died in 1987 at age 86. At 22 he published *Dadaisuto Shinkichi no Shi* (The Poems of Dadaist Shinkichi) and became the first Dadaist poet in Japan. When young he lived as a monk in a Shingon Buddhist temple, but later turned passionately to Zen Buddhism. His renown as "the Zen poet" even spread abroad. Many of his poems seize a Zen moment and instantly fly to the heart of the object.

The title of this three-line poem, which is one of his most famous, is *Rusu* (I'm Out). To escape everyday time and space at a stroke—this is poetry's magic, and these few lines possess it.

頭に遊ぶは頭虱
Kōbe ni asobu wa kashira-jirami

項の窩をぞ極めて食ふ
Unaji no kubo wa zo kimete kuu

櫛の歯より天降る
Kushi no ha yori amakudaru

麻筍の蓋にて命終はる
Ogoke no futa nite mei owaru

梁塵秘抄
Ryōjin Hishō

Head-lice play upon the head
and always nibble at the neck,
then from the comb descend to earth,
to end their lives on a hemp-box lid

Among the popular songs of daily life in the Heian period, this tale of the life of a louse is one of the most unusual.

Unaji no kubo means the depression at the base of the skull, where it meets the neck. *Kimete* means always, constantly. *Amakudaru* originally meant a god coming down to earth, and now means taking early retirement from a government job to a private company; but here it is used for the lice, who "descend" from the "heaven" of the head after being caught in a fine-toothed comb. *Ogoke* is a container for hemp, on the lid of which the lice, crushed between nail and lid, end their lives. There is an interesting spatial movement from above to below.

旅人の
Tabibito no

宿りせむ野に
yadori semu no ni

霜降らば
shimo furaba

わが子羽ぐくめ
waga ko hagukume

天の鶴群
ama no tazumura

遣唐使随員の母
Kentōshi zui-in no Haha

If frost falls on the fields
where the travellers sleep,
enfold my child
in your wings,
cranes of the sky above
    Mother of a member of the embassy to China

Man'yōshū, Book 9. In early summer of 733, Ambassdor to China Tajihi no Hironari and his retinue departed from Naniwa (now Osaka), to return in 735.

When they departed, a mother praying for her child's safety wrote this poem. Thinking how cold he would be as he travelled over the fields of a far-off land through the autumn and winter, she appealed to the cranes in the sky.

The traditional Chinese idea of the night crane who devotes herself wholly to nurturing her chicks, never leaving her nest, may be in the background, but maternal feelings transcend national boundaries.

十字街頭乞食しをはり
Jūji gaitō kotsujiki shiowari

八幡宮辺を方に徘徊す
Hachimangū hen wo masani haikai su

児童相見てともに相語る
Jidō aimite tomo ni aikataru

去年の癡僧今また来たりと
Kyonen no chisō ima mata kitari to

良寛
Ryōkan

After begging for food at crossings
and roadsides
now I wander around Hachiman Shrine
The children look at each other and say
"That crazy monk from last year—
he's back again"

From *Ryōkan Dōjin Ikō*. Ryōkan was the eldest
son of a Shinto priest from Izumozaki in the prov-
ince of Echigo, but he became a Zen monk in his
early twenties. There may have been some dra-
matic reason, now unknown, for this coversion
from Shinto to Zen.

Ryōkan revered the famous Zen priest Kokusen
Oshō and went all the way to Bitchū province (now
Okayama Prefecture) to study under him. After
travelling throughout western and eastern Japan
in pursuit of enlightenment for many years, he
returned to Echigo in his late forties and entered
the Gogōan, a hermitage on Mt. Kugami.

This poem, originally in Chinese, describes a
scene from his mendicant life. The children may
seem to be mocking him, but of course they spoke
from affection.

黒猿は子を抱きて坐して
法を聞き

Kokuen wa ko wo idakite zashite
　hō wo kiki

青鹿は群を呼びて
跪きて花を献ず

seiroku wa gun wo yobite
　hizamazukite hana wo kenzu

明極楚俊

Minki Soshun

A black monkey cradles her baby
as she sits and listens to the law
A pale deer calls his fellows
and kneeling offers flowers

From *Gozan Bungaku Shū, Edo Kanshi Shū*. Soshun was a Chinese Zen priest of the Yuan dynasy. In his later years he crossed the sea to Japan, was revered by Emperor Godaigo and became head priest successively of the temples of Kenchōji, Nanzenji and Kenninji.

Gozan Bungaku or Literature of the Five Mountains is usually used as a general term for the poetry and prose written by native Japanese Zen monks of the five large Rinzai temples in Kamakura and Kyoto, but among them were Chinese monks like Soshun too.

This is one stanza of a *shichi-gon risshi*, a Chinese poem of eight lines, each line seven characters long. Its title is *Sankyo* (Mountain Life). As a monk is reading the sutras aloud, a black monkey and a pale deer come and humbly listen. The poem celebrates life at a mountain temple, rich in its simplicity.

寂しさは
Sabishisa wa

その色としも
sono iro to shimo

なかりけり
nakarikeri

真木立つ山の
Maki tatsu yama no

秋の夕暮れ
aki no yūgure

寂蓮法師
Jakuren Hōshi

Loneliness is not
a single
color
Cypress covered mountains
in the autumn dusk
Priest Jakuren

Shinkokinshū, Book 4, Autumn. The first of the so-called "Three evening poems," which see at the bottom of autumn's loneliness a beauty even deeper than ordinary beauty.

Maki is a general term for evergreens like cypress and cryptomeria. The phrase "autumn colors" usually brings to mind bright red and yellow leaves. But here evergreens stand silently on a mountain in the autumn dusk and the poet, seeing in them a loneliness whose source he can neither pinpoint nor define, is struck by a profound and mysterious beauty.

芋嵐
Imoarashi

猫が髭張り
Neko ga hige hari

歩きをり
arukiori

村山古郷
Murayama Kokyō

Taro wind—
whiskers extended,
the cat walks on

From *Murayama Kokyō Shū*, 1980. Haiku poet and critic born 1909 in Kyoto, died 1986 in Tokyo. He began writing haiku under the guidance of his elder brother Kikyō, also a haiku poet. Respected for the breadth of his knowledge of modern haiku history and its groups, he published many books in those areas too.

Imoarashi is the strong autumn wind that blows the taro leaves back so that their white undersides show. When this wind blows, the kittens born in early summer are turning into handsome adult cats. The sight of them walking, whiskers extended, on the paths through the fields, with that special dignity cats have, has *okashimi* or the humor characteristic of haiku.

眼耳双つながら忘れて
Ganji futatsu nagara wasurete

身も亦失ひ
mi mo mata ushinai

空中に独り唱ふ白雲の吟
kuchū ni hitori utau haku-un no gin

夏目漱石
Natsume Sōseki

Eyes and ears forgotten,
body gone,
alone in the air, I sing of white clouds

Sōseki Zenshū. The last lines of *Mudai* (Untitled), a Chinese poem in the *shichigon risshi* form (eight lines, seven characters each). Sōseki wrote it on the night of November 20, 1916, and died on December 9 of the same year.

This work is the last of his Chinese poems, which are an important part of the works of his last years, going far beyond an intellectual hobby or efforts at cultural improvement. Taking his themes from his own inner world, Sōseki spoke freely of life in universal terms, and in that sense created modern style poems using the traditional forms of Chinese poetry. The shadow of death hovers over this last work, but in the strength and clarity of its language it is one with his earlier writings.

木枯の
Kogarashi no

地にも落さぬ
chi ni mo otosanu

しぐれかな
shigure kana

向井去来
Mukai Kyorai

Chill rain,
caught up in winter's gale,
lightly skims the earth

From *Kyorai Hokku Shū*. Bashō's comments on this poem in *Kyorai Shō* have made it famous. Bashō compared it to one by Kakei, another follower of his: "Will the two-day moon / blow away, scattered / by the winter wind?" (*Kogarashi ni futsuka no tsuki no fukichiru ka*). He said that Kakei's poem merely juxtaposed the sliver-thin two-day old moon with the fierce winter wind. There was nothing special about Kyorai's poem, on the other hand, but somehow all its parts worked together very well. The only fault he found was the original *chi made* (all the way to earth), which he had Kyorai change to *chi ni mo* (even to the earth).

This anecdote exemplifies what subtle but strong effects prepositions have in Japanese.

大鳥の羽根に　ヤレナ
Ōtori no hane ni yarena

霜降れり　ヤレナ
shimo fureri yarena

誰かさ言ふ
Tare ka sa iu

千鳥ぞさ言ふ
Chidori zo sa iu

鶛ぞさ言ふ
Kayaguki zo sa iu

蒼鷺ぞ　京より来てさ言ふ
Mitosagi zo miyako yori kite sa iu

風俗歌
Fuzoku Uta

Frost fell, la-la
on the big birds' wings, la-la
Who says so?
The plover says,
the sparrow says
The heron, come from Miyako, says

Unlike lyric poetry, with its intense expression of personal feeling, folk songs always have more than one person, and usually several, behind them. It follows that they often take dialogue form. This is one example, with *Tara ka sa iu* (Who says so?) being the other person's inter-linear question.

In Miyako (literally, the capital, that is, Kyoto) the frost has already fallen on the big birds' wings and it's getting cold—so say the little birds who have come to the country. This sort of poem has its own artless humor.

君かへす
Kimi kaesu

朝の鋪石
asa no shiki-ishi

さくさくと
saku-saku to

雪よ林檎の
Yuki yo ringo no

香のごとくふれ
ka no gotoku fure

北原　白秋
Kitahara Hakushū

I send you home in the morning
the snowy path crunching
under your feet
Oh snow, fall
with the scent of apples!

From *Kiri no Hana* (Paulownia Flowers, 1913). In the late Meiji period, Hakushū had defined a new era in modern poetry with his collections *Jashūmon* and *Omoide*; with *Kiri no Hana* he became a central figure in tanka as well. This was not only because of its new style, but also because of the revolution (recorded in the "Poems of Sorrow" section of *Kiri no Hana*) in his personal life that followed his arrest due to his love affair with a married woman. As he wrote: "A snowy night, / we draw near the red hearth, / another's wife and I— / where can we go / from here?" (*Yuki no yo no akaki irori ni suriyoritsu hitozuma to ware to nan to subekemu*). But the real newness of his style was in poems like the first one above, with its inborn sensual freshness and effortless luminosity.

星を数ふれば七つ、
Hoshi wo kazoureba nanatsu,

金の灯台は九つ、
kin no tōdai wa kokonotsu

岩陰に白き牡蠣かぎりなく
Iwakage ni shiroki kaki kagirinaku

生るれど、
umaruredo,

わが恋はひとつにして
Waga koi wa hitotsu ni shite

寂し。
sabishi.

西条八十
Saijō Yaso

Count the stars: there are seven.
And of gold lighthouses, nine.
In the shadows of the rocks,
white oysters breed, infinitudes,
but of my love there is but one, alone

From *Sakin* (Gold Dust, 1919). Yaso, who was born in 1892 in Tokyo and died in 1970, was very famous as a lyricist for children's songs, popular songs and military songs. His works traced the subtle movements of the heart with a delicate and sensitive sense of language; he was one of ten central figures among the so-called "Artistic" poets of the Taishō period.

This is the short poem "*Umi ni te*" (By the sea) in its entirety. "Seven", "nine", "infinitudes", and "of my love there is but one"—the fulcrum is the placement and contrast of numerals as he sings of love and nostalgia. With his clear-cut style, he revivified a technique sometimes found in old folk songs.

生きながら
Ikinagara

針に貫かれし
hari ni nukareshi

蝶のごとく
chō no gotoku

悶へつつなお
modaetsutsu nao

飛ばむとぞする
tobamu to zo suru

原　阿佐緒
Hara Asao

Alive but
pierced with pins
a butterfly
in torment still
I try to fly

From *Ruikon* (Tear Traces, 1923). A tanka poet who was born in 1888 in Miyagi Prefecture and died in 1969. She originally meant to be a painter in the traditional Japanese style, but caught up by tanka and encouraged by Yosano Akiko, joined the New Poetry Society. She later changed to the Araragi group, but was expelled because of a scandalous love affair. The rest of her life was also filled with troubles.

The poem expresses the suffering and pride of a woman who tried to live in complete fidelity to her own nature in an age when to do so meant inevitable collisions with the prevailing social mores.

雪の日の
Yuki no hi no

浴身一指
Yokushin isshi

一趾愛し
isshi kanashi

橋本多佳子
Hashimoto Takako

A snowy day
a bath in my body
each finger each toe dear

From *Myōjū* (Life's End, 1965), her post-humous collection of haiku. This poem appears at the end of the collection, together with "Fierce snow / So many the words / I leave behind". (*Yuki hage-shi Kaki-nokosu koto nan zo ōki*). It is about taking a bath the day before she entered hospital for the last time.

Outside there is snow. She washes each finger and each toe with special care. A grave illness has ensconced itself within her; the premonition that she will be parting with her body soon arouses an infinite tenderness.

Takako's poems, with their precise expression and freshness of feeling, possess a strong sense of individuality.

燈影なき室に我あり
Hokage naki shitsu ni ware ari

父と母
Chichi to haha

壁のなかより杖つきて出づ
kabe no naka yori tsue tsukite izu

石川啄木
Ishikawa Takuboku

I am in
a lightless room
Father and Mother
leaning on canes
step out from the wall

From *Ichiaku no Suna* (A Handful of Sand, 1910). After years of wandering around Hokkaidō, Takuboku came to Tokyo in 1908 and made an all-or-nothing effort to succeed as a writer. When he failed, even his hope of bringing his wife and child, whom he had left in Hakodate in the care of his friend, Miyazaki Ikuu, fell through. In the midst of his irritation and despair came a sudden outpouring of tanka—141 poems in one night of late June. This is one of them.

Far off, a mother and father patiently await the return of their son. But in the darkness of his rented room, the son sadly stares at the wall until the apparitions of his parents emerge from it.

人老いぬ
Hito oinu

人又我を
Hito mata ware wo

老と呼
rō to yobu

蕪 村
Buson

泥に尾を引く
Doro ni o wo hiku

亀のやすさよ
kame no yasusa yo

樗 良
Chora

He's gotten old—
and now he calls me
"dear old man"

Giant turtle drags its tail
in the mud, happy and slow

From *Ichiya Yon Kasen, Kono Hotori*. One night Buson, Kito and Chora visited Wada Ranzan, who was sick at his home in Kyoto's Oil Alley, and the four friends spent the night composing linked verse. Working at fever pitch, they completed four chains of linked verse in a night; this verse is the last part of the second chain.

Buson's link, which says that his friend and he have both reached an age when they can be called "old", is followed by Chora's, which compares peaceful old age to an ancient turtle happily dragging its tail in the mud, so ending the chain on a felicitous note.

The turtle image is borrowed from an anecdote in the chapter "Autumn Water" of *The Book of Chuang-tzu*, a classic text of Chinese philosophy.

心がうらぶれたときは
Kokoro ga urabur: toki wa

音楽を聞くな。
ongaku wo kiku na.

空気と水と石ころ
Kūki to mizu to ishikoro

ぐらいしかない所へ
gurai shika nai tokoro e

そっと沈黙を食べに行け！
sotto chinmoku wo tabe ni ike !

清岡卓行
Kiyooka Takayuki

When your heart's in ruins, never listen to music.
Go off someplace where there's nothing but air, water and stones,
and make a quiet meal of silence !

From *Shiki no Suketchi* (Sketches of the Four Seasons, 1966). The author is a poet and prose writer born in Dairen, China, 1922. This is the first two and a half lines of the four line poem *Mimi wo tsūjite* (Through the ears). The last lines are: "Because from the distance come / echoes of the words that will help you live" (*Tōku kara ikiru tame no kotoba ga, kodama shite kuru kara*).

The poet is saying not to seek solace in music when one is depressed, but rather to go into the wilds and quietly eat silence. There is no paradox here. You give yourself up to sadness and await the rebirth of the necessary words. Kiyooka, by the way, as is evident from his poems and stories, loves music.

ふじの山
Fuji no yama

夢に見るこそ
yume ni miru koso

果報なれ
kahō nare

路銀もいらず
Rogin mo irazu

草臥もせず
kutabire mo sezu

油煙斎永田貞柳
Yuensai Nagata Teiryū

*To dream of
Mount Fuji—
now that's good luck!
It's free, and you save
your feet.*

From *Teiryū-ō Kyōka Zenshū*. The satiric verse form called *kyōka* reached its peak in Edo of the 1780s, but about a century earlier, in Osaka, we find this practitioner of the form, who was famous among his fellow poets everywhere in Japan. He was born into a family that had been confection makers for generations, but his father wrote haiku and *kyōka* and there were also haiku poets among his uncles. His younger brother was the *jōruri* playwright Ki no Kaion.

This poem gives a humorous twist to the common belief that the appearance of Mount Fuji, a hawk or an eggplant in your first dream of the new year brings good luck. Dreaming of Mount Fuji is lucky, it says, because you are spared the expense and exhaustion of actually going there.

冬木だち
Fuyu kodachi

月骨髄に
tsuki kotsuzui ni

入夜哉
iru yo kana

　　几董
　　Kitō

Winter trees—
The moon shines into
my marrow tonight

此句老杜が
Kono ku Rōto ga

寒き腸
samuki harawata

　　蕪村
　　Buson

This poem—Old Tu's
frozen insides

From *Momo Sumomo* (Peach and Plum). Takai Kitō was one of Yosa Buson's chief disciples. These poems were the first and second links in a linked-verse sequence they made by letter.

The first link describes a night when the moon shines so clear and cold through the winter trees that it seems to pass through the bones and light up your very marrow. In the second link, Buson responds with praise for the pathos of Kitō's poem, which reminds him, he says, of the extreme starkness of the Chinese poet Tu Fu. "Old Tu" is used to distinguish Tu Fu from Tu Mu, or "Little Tu", another poet of the T'ang period.

The taut, condensed style, learned from Chinese poetry, achieves a striking clarity of scene and emotion.

ふるさとに
Furusato ni

行く人もがな
yuku hito mogana

告げやらむ
Tsugeyaramu

知らぬ山路に
Shiranu yamaji ni

ひとりまどふと
hitori madou to

後一条院中宮亡霊
Go-ichijō-in Chūgū Bōrei

Oh, for someone to go to my old home
and tell them all
how on these mountain paths
I wander alone and
lost !

Ghost of the Consort of Retired Emperor Go-Ichijō

Shinkokinshū, Book 8, Laments. The author was Fujiwara Michinaga's daughter Ishi. She died young, but according to the headnote, she appeared in someone's dream and recited this poem before the grief of those she left behind had had time to heal.

"Old home" usually means one's birthplace, but here, used by one who is dead, means this world. The meaning, then, is: If only there were someone going from the world of the dead to the world of the living, I'd have them tell those still alive of the pain of wandering in the next world.

It was not unheard of in those days for a ghost to appear in someone's dream and make some appeal. That is why the purpose of memorial services was to ease the dead in their journey through the next world.

暁や
Akatsuki ya

鯨の吼ゆる
Kujira no hoyuru

しもの海
shimo no umi

加藤暁台
Katō Kyōtai

At day break
on frost-white seas
the whales roar

From *Kyōtai Kushū*. A haiku poet who ranked with Buson in the middle Edo Period, during the haikai revival. Born in Nagoya, at one time he served the branch of the Tokugawa family that lived in Owari. There was a unique quality of liveliness in his way of observing objects.

Frost has settled everywhere on the sea, bleak and cold. In the chill quiet of dawn, whales are energetically shooting their spray up into the air. *Hoyuru* means this shooting up of the spray. The poem is imaginary but the image is captivating, and the words have a cheerful, rollicking rhythm.

冬の夢の
Fuyu no yume no

おどろきはつる
odoroki hatsuru

曙に
akebono ni

春のうつつの
haru no utsutsu no

まづ見るゆるかな
mazu miyuru kana

藤原良経
Fujiwara Yoshitsune

Winter dreams,
   surprised, break off—
      it's dawn!
Before my eyes
   is spring's reality

From *Akishino Gessei Shū*. Yoshitsune, Regent and Grand Minister Go-Kyōgoku, died suddenly at age 37. He studied poetry with Fujiwara Shunzei and Shunzei's son Teika, and was a strong supporter of their style. His own was the most limpid and elegant of all the poets in the *Shinkokinshū*.

In classical Japanese, *odoroku*, "surprised", means to wake up with a start.

The symmetrically juxtaposed winter/spring and dream/reality evoke with skill and beauty the joy of the passing of winter and the coming of spring. As the speaker awakes with a start from a winter's dream, he sees the true body of spring in the shape of a spring dawn.

東風吹くや
Kochi fuku ya

耳現はるゝ
Mimi arawaruru

うなゐ髪
unaigami

杉田久女
Sugita Hisajo

East winds blow—
ears emerge from
nape-length hair

From *Sugita Hisajo Kushū*, 1952. Of the many women haiku poets in Takahama Kyoshi's haiku group, Hisajo was by far the most talented, but in her later years ill health and psychological stress destroyed her. Masako Ishi, Hisajo's oldest daughter, now devotes herself to refuting the many slanderous stories that have grown up about her mother; this poem from Hisajo's early period may be about Masako's childhood.

Unaigami is what we call *okappagami* now, a short bob worn by children. When the east wind gently blows, the girl's adorable ears appear from beneath her hair. The child's innocence and the classical elegance of the words intensify each other.

たくあんの
Takuan no

波利と音して
hari to oto shite

梅ひらく
ume hiraku

加藤楸邨
Katō Shūson

The crunch of
pickled radish—
plum blossoms open

From *Fukkoshi*, 1976. Should the characters 波利 be read *hari* or *pari*? *Pari* is closer to the true sound the radish makes when someone bites into it, but even so I think the characters should be read as *hari*. The poet has deliberately written the word with kanji, which leaves room for both readings, as if he were lightly juggling the two possibilities. With the mind so opened, the phrase "plum blossoms open" can resonate gently against the pickly crunch.

Being able to see pickles and plum blossoms linked in this way is one of the ambrosial delights of reading poetry.

朝づく日
Asazuku hi

向ひの山に
mukai no yama ni

月立てり見ゆ
tsuki tateri miyu

遠妻を
Tōzuma wo

持ちたる人し
mochitaru hito shi

見つつ偲はむ
mitsutsu shinobamu

柿本人麻呂歌集
Kakinomoto no
Hitomaro Kashū

Above the mountain facing me
like the morning sun,
I see the newly risen moon
A man with wife far off
must be gazing long
and yearning

Man'yōshū, Book 7. A *sedōka*, or poem of six lines arranged in two verses of 5-7-7 syllables each. *Asazuku hi*, "the morning sun", is a pillow word for *mukai*, "facing", perhaps from the image of turning toward the rising sun. A pillow word does not function in terms of its literal meaning, so there is no contradiction between the morning sun and the evening moon. *Shi* is an emphatic particle.

The poem takes place at evening, as the speaker watches the rising moon appear over the mountain ahead. He imagines a traveler who has left his wife behind and thinks of her with longing while gazing at the moon. The word *tōzuma*, "distant wife", gives the poem a particular charm.

紙雛や
Kamibina ya

恋したさうな
koi shitasō na

顔ばかり
kao bakari

正岡子規
Masaoka Shiki

Paper dolls—
each with a face
made for love

From *Kanzan Rakuboku*, a work of 1896. The Dolls' Festival (March 3) is ancient in origin. It is thought that the dolls used in it can be traced back to the paper dolls used in Shinto prayers and purification ceremonies. In medieval times, the festival dolls, like Shinto ceremonial ones, were thrown into the river or the ocean after the holiday was over. This similarity suggests that paper dolls for the Dolls' Festival were probably the earliest form.

Among the many haiku, traditional and modern, about the Dolls' Festival, Shiki's is rather unusual. The language and tone are straightforward and unadorned, but there is a kind of overflowing affection for the dolls, whose captivating expressions suggest they would speak if they could.

春の日や
Haru no hi ya

あの世この世と
Anoyo konoyo to

馬車を駆り
basha wo kari

中村苑子
Nakamura Sonoko

Spring day—
Between that world and this
I drive my horse-drawn carriage

From *Suiyō Shikan*, 1975. Nakamura Sonoko has also written: "In Hades / I still comb my hair— / the loneliness" (*Yomi ni kite mada kami suku wa sabishi-kere*). She is forever going in and out of an unreal world that the ordinary methods of realism and natural description almost never touch on. But while "that world" is undoubtedly unreal, the human heart it-self is always freely and miraculously crossing and recrossing such boundaries.

On a hushed spring day, with something mad and magical in the air, she rides back and forth between this world and the world of the dead, driving herself in an old-fashioned horse-drawn carriage.

樹脂の香に
Jushi no ka ni

朝は悩まし
asa wa nayamashi

うしなひし
Ushinaishi

さまざまのゆめ、
samazama no yume,

森竝は
Morinami wa

風に鳴るかな
kaze ni naru kana

中原中也
Nakahara Chūya

Morning aches   with resin's scent
Various   lost dreams,
Forests whistle   in the wind

From *Yagi no Uta*, 1935. The third stanza of a 14 line poem written in the literary language and called *Asa no Uta* (Morning Song), composed when the author was 19 and which he himself considered his first real poem.

It is written from the point of view of a young man lying in bed, just awake, as the sights, sounds and smells of the outer world reach him. The ennui that was already Chūya's trademark is all-pervasive and yet in the line "Morning aches with resin's scent", the energy of youth still asserts itself.

核弾頭
Kakudantō

五万個秘めて
gomanko himete

藍色の
ai-iro no

天空に浮く
tenkū ni uku

われらが地球
warera ga chikyū

加藤克巳
Katō Katsumi

50,000 nuclear warheads
tucked away, it drifts
in indigo space:
our
earth

From *Katō Katsumi Zenkashū*, 1985. Born in Kyoto in 1915, Katsumi published his first collection of tanka in 1937, while still in college. In such poems as "A pure white arm / stretches down / from the sky. / My brain unravels / in morning ecstasy" (*Masshiroi ude ga sora kara nobite kuru Nukareyuku nōzui no kesa no kaikan*) he showed his affinity for the New Sensationalist novelists of the 1920s. His pursuit of fresh sensation has continued with his most recent works, like this one. It is like looking at an illustration in a science magazine, but the image is permeated by a pathos characteristic of the tanka.

俎や
Manaita ya

青菜で拭ふ
Aona de nuguu

烏賊の墨
ika no sumi

松瀬青々
Matsuse Seisei

The cutting board—
squid ink mopped up
with greens

From *Tsumaki*, 1905. Seisei studied haiku under Masaoka Shiki in Tokyo, but afterward returned to Osaka, his birthplace, and became editor of the Osaka *Asahi Shimbun's* haiku page. A central figure in haiku circles in western Japan, he also drew haiku pictures. He was a man of many pleasures, one of which was, apparently, good food. His poems have the same flavor as the refined cuisine of western Japan. This one talks directly about the food itself with a detail and sharpness of image that conveys the physical sensation of wiping up the thick cuttlefish ink.

行く春や
Yuku haru ya

海を見て居る
Umi wo mite iru

鴉の子
karasu no ko

有井諸九
Arii Shokyū

Spring goes by—
crow's child scans
the sea

From *Shokyū-Ni Kushū*. The most famous example of a woman of good family who awoke after an arranged marriage and eloped with her lover is Yanagihara Byakuren, who was born into the nobility. But there were such women even in premodern times of course, and the author of this poem was one. Born into a well-off family of Chikugo in Kyūshū, Shokyū married a relative, but later eloped with Arii Fufū, a disciple of Yaba, himself one of Bashō's favorite disciples. Fond of traveling, she observed nature with fresh eyes, as in this poem, and became a well-known haiku poet in the 18th century. After her husband died, she shaved her head and became a Buddhist nun.

おぼつかな鳥だに鳴かぬ奥山に
Obotsukana tori dani nakanu okuyama ni

人こそ音すなれ
hito koso oto su nare

あな尊
Ana tōto

修行者の通るなりけり
Shugyōja no tōru narikeri

梁塵秘抄
Ryōjin Hishō

In deep and lonely mountains
where even birds don't cry
suddenly, a human sound
Ah, wonderful—
A holy man is passing by

At *oto su nare* there is a pause, followed by the exclamation *ana tōto*. The speaker has ventured into mountains so high and remote that even birds are absent. Suddenly, the rustle of human footsteps breaks the intense loneliness and before the speaker's fright-stiffened frame can relax, a mountain ascetic has walked swiftly by. Thus the exclamation, "Ah, wonderful." The unadorned description of an emotional tremor became a brief ballad.

わかき身の
Wakaki mi no

かかる嘆きに
kakaru nageki ni

世を去ると
yo wo saru to

思はで経にし
omowade henishi

日も遠きかな
hi mo tōki kana

山川登美子
Yamakawa Tomiko

I was young
and never thought I'd leave
the world with this regret
in those days
long ago

Myōjo, May 1908. Tomiko was praised, with Akiko Yosano, as the finest flower of the New Poetry Society, but her brief life was brought to a close by tuberculosis in the spring of 1909, when she was only 30. She stared unblinking at her own death in poems like: "My coffin, without anyone / to watch over it, / passes through the fields . . . / I see its loneliness / amid the drifting mists" (*Waga hitsugi mamoru hito naku yuku nobe no sabishisa mietsu kasumi tanabiku*); but she also felt the grief and bitterness expressed so intensely in the poem above. The echo of despair is especially strong in the last line's *tōki kana*, "long ago".

頭の中で
Atama no naka de

白い夏野と
shiroi natsuno to

なってゐる
natte iru

高屋窓秋
Takaya Sōshū

The inside of my head
has become
a white summer field

Shiroi Natsuno, 1936. The first character would be read as *zu* if the 5-7-5 structure of haiku were observed, and some critics do so; but the author himself has said that he reads it as *atama*. The poem's center is in the image "white summer field" and reading the first character with the Chinese reading of *zu* would have given the first word an undesirable heaviness.

Sōshū was a favorite disciple of Mizuhara Shūōshi. In 1932, when he composed this poem, it opened new possibilities for the young haiku poets who were trying to reconstruct the haiku by departing from objective realism and natural description. In this sense, the poem has historical significance; it was widely discussed as one of Sōshū's most important early works.

卯の花に
U no hana ni

蘆毛の馬の
ashige no uma no

夜明哉
yoake kana

森川許六
Morikawa Kyoriku

Deutzia flowers
and a dappled horse
at dawn

From *A Sack of Charcoal*. Titled "On a trip."

Kyoriku, a disciple of Bashō's last years, was a samurai of the 300-*koku* fief of Hikone and a man of many talents. This poem seems to have been written on his way back to Hikone from Edo in early May, 1693. The poem's center is the juxtaposition of the horse's black and brown speckled whiteness with the fresh white of the flowers by the side of the road. The time is dawn, and the mood of early summer permeates the scene. This reminds me: I have yet to find a modern haiku which treats the everyday modern event of setting off on a trip—not by horse at dawn, of course, but by car—in this refreshing way.

苗売の
Nae-uri no

声が巷より
koe ga chimata yori

透るなり
tōru nari

壁に耳あて
Kabe ni mimi ate

なつかしなつかし
natsukashi natsukashi

小名木綱夫
Onagi Tsunao

The seedling vendor's voice
penetrates from
the street
Suffused with longing
I press my ear to the wall

Taiko, 1949. Nowadays one almost never hears the voice of the street vendor of eggplant, gourds and other seedlings in early summer. Street vendors of any sort, in fact, are near extinction, and even when they appear, the voice is almost always a prerecorded loudspeaker message.

This poem was written during World War II, when the author's tanka poems brought him under suspicion and he was imprisoned under the Peace Preservation Law. He listens to the vendor's voice with his ear pressed against the prison wall, feeling unbearable nostalgia for life on the outside. The poem is straight-forward and affecting.

After the war, Onagi joined the Communist Party and worked as a reporter for *Akahata*, the party newspaper. He died of tuberculosis at age 38.

かへり来ぬ
Kaerikonu

むかしを今と
mukashi wo ima to

おもひ寝の
omoine no

夢の枕に
yume no makura ni

匂ふたちばな
niou tachibana

式子内親王
Shikishi Naishinnō

I slept to make
the past, forever gone,
into the now,
and to the pillow where I dreamt
came the scent of orange blossoms

Shinkokinshū, Book 3, Summer. In the world of classical Japanese poetry, certain very fleeting sense perceptions evoked strong poetic associations. One of the best examples was the scent of orange blossoms. "In the fragrance / of the fifth month / orange blossoms, / I smell the scented sleeves / of a person of the past" (*Satsuki matsu hana tachibana no ka wo kageba mukashi no hito no sode no ka zo suru*). This poem from the *Kokinshū* forever associated the scent of orange blossoms with happy days of past love. Alluding to that shared perception, Shikishi Naishinnō created a lovely poem about nostalgia, as delicate as the blossoms' scent itself.

牡丹散て
Botan chirite

打ちかさなりぬ
uchi-kasanarinu

二三片
ni san pen

与謝蕪村
Yosa Buson

Peony petals fall,
pile up—
two or three

Buson Kushū. The effect of the poem as a whole makes one want to read the third character as *chitte*, but Buson himself wrote it out in a letter as *chirite*. Even so, *chitte* has its own attractions.

The Chinese called the peony, with its large blossoms, the emperor of flowers; and from the 17th century on, the Japanese cultivated it devotedly as an ornamental flower. The clarity and firmness of *uchi-kasanarinu* / *ni san pen*, "pile up— / two or three", captures perfectly both aspects of the fallen petals— their heroic purity and their sensual charm.

ほとゝぎす
Hototogisu

自由自在に
jiyū jizai ni

きく里は
kiku sato wa

酒屋へ三里
sakaya e san ri

豆腐屋へ二里
tōfuya e ni ri

頭　光
Tsumuri no Hikaru (Shiny Head)

From the village
where you hear the cuckoo
to your heart's content
it's three miles to the nearest liquor
and two to the tofu store

Bandai Kyōka Shū. A *kyōka* or satiric tanka, about that summer symbol, the Japanese cuckoo. Come summer, everyone writes poems about the cuckoo to show how cultured they are. But very few bother to go to the best places for hearing its song, which are always out-of-the-way villages, far from such comforts of civilization as the liquor store and the tofu maker. The target of the poem's iconoclastic laughter is clear on a single reading, making this one of the best satiric tanka.

Judging from the pen name Shiny Head, the author must have lost his hair rather young. He was an urban official, and also a famous *kyōka* poet.

垢なりや塵なりや是何物なりや
Aka nari ya Chiri nari ya Kore nani mono nari ya

元来見来れば更に無骨なり
Ganrai mi kitareba sara ni bukotsu nari

一休宗純
Ikkyū Sōjun

What's this—Old skin? Dust?

A close look tells all—boneless freaks.

Edo Kanshi Shū. Ikkyū, that great priest of the Muromachi period, also wrote wonderful Chinese poetry, both serious and satiric. These are the first two lines of a four-line satiric poem from *Ikkyū Shokoku Monogatari* (Tales of Ikkyū's Travels). It is titled *Nomi ni daisu* (On Fleas), and the last two lines go: "They've grown fat on human flesh/ but this thin priest can do them in with a single pinch." (*Hito wo kuraite jūbun ni koetari to iedomo sōsō no hitohineri ni mo shōgai wo bossen*). Was the flea a means to protest the immoral power and vain glory he saw around him?

うすものの
Usumono no

二尺のたもと
nishaku no tamoto

すべりおちて
suberi ochite

蛍ながるる
hotaru nagaruru

夜風の青き
yokaze no aoki

与謝野晶子
Yosano Akiko

Down silken sleeve
two feet long
fireflies glide and slide,
then flow into
the evening breeze's green

Midaregami, 1901. Akiko liked to weave numbers into her poems: "hair five feet long", "a three-foot boat", "a thousand strands of hair", "a twenty-year-old wife" are a few examples. In the hands of a skillful poet, such usage can add clarity to the poem's images.

Like shining drops, fireflies slide down the long sleeves of a young girl's thin summer kimono, then fly off. The evening breeze is so fresh it seems green. Now such a scene almost seems like a dream from a lost world.

心凄きもの
Kokoro sugoki mono

夜道船道
Yomichi funamichi

旅の空
Tabi no sora

旅の宿
Tabi no yado

木闇き山寺の経の声
Koguraki yamadera no kyō no koe

想ふや仲らひの飽かで退く
Omou ya nakarai no akade noku

梁塵秘抄
Ryōjin Hishō

Things that cast a shadow on the heart:
Night paths, ocean roads,
the sky while traveling,
travelers' inns
A single voice chanting sutras,
at a mountain temple dark with trees
A loving couple parting,
filled with desire

Kokoro sugoki means "chilled, forlorn, terribly lonely". This poem is a list of things which evoke such feelings. *Funamichi* means "sea voyage", and the *sora* of *tabi no sora* means "state of mind" as well as "sky". The *ya* of *omou ya* is an interjection for the sake of rhythm. *Akade* means "before the heart is fully satisfied". The move at the very end, from the realm of the concrete to the world of the heart, is beautifully done.

新月や
Shingetsu ya

蛸壺に目が
Takotsubo ni me ga

生える頃
haeru koro

佐藤鬼房
Satō Onifusa

New moon—
when octopus pots
sprout eyes

Izuko e, 1984. No haiku poet writing about octopus traps can ignore Basho's famous haiku on the subject: "Octopus pots— / Fleeting dreams, / a summer moon" (*Takotsubo ya Hakanaki yume wo natsu no tsuki*). This haiku by Onifusa, a contemporary poet, also juxtaposes octopus pots to the moon, but with a thoroughly modern sensibility. The eyes, of course, belong to the octopuses that have crawled into the pot, but with the phrase *me ga haeru*, "sprout eyes", the poem acquires both an animated, lighthearted quality and the feel of a surrealist painting.

月てらす
Tsuki terasu

河を踰えつつ
kawa wo koetsutsu

ししむらの
shishimura no

うちなる鳥も
uchinaru tori mo

目をひらきをり
me wo hirakiori

高野公彦
Takano Kimihiko

I cross

the moon-lit river,
the eyes of the bird
within my body

open wide

Tansei (Faint Blue, 1982). The characters for *shishimura*, which means "body", are 肉叢. Cutting across a river bathed in moonlight, the poet has a sudden sense of awakening. To express it, he invents a bird dwelling within his body who opens its eyes. A kind of sensuous, yet internal, imaginative power is hard at work here. One sees this kind of fantastical conception rather often among young tanka poets these days. Done without thought, it can seem merely deliberate mystification, but here that trap is avoided.

白壁を
Shirakabe wo

隔てて病める
hedatete yameru

をとめらの
otomera no

或る時は脈を
aru toki wa myaku wo

とりあふ声す
toriau koe su

相良宏
Sagara Hiroshi

Through the white wall
at times I hear
the feverish virgins' voices
as they measure
each other's pulses

Sagara Hiroshi Kashū, 1956. A tanka poet born in Tokyo in 1925, Sagara died of tuberculosis of the lungs in 1955. Near the end of World War II, he entered a technical institute to study aircraft engineering, but becoming ill, withdrew and spent the rest of his life in a sanatorium. Next to his room was one for young women patients. When they took each other's pulses, their voices, raised now in surprise, now in laughter, could be heard through the white sickroom wall.

A lonely, yet lively feeling saturates this poem's precise expression. Its author's early end can only be lamented.

もゆる限りは
Moyuru kagiri wa

ひとに与へし
hito ni ataeshi

乳房なれ
chibusa nare

癌の組成を
Gan no sosei wo

何時よりと知らず
itsu yori to shirazu

中城ふみ子
Nakajō Fumiko

As long as they blazed
I gave to him
my breasts
and never knew when
the cancer took on shape

Chibusa Soshitsu, **1954.** There are poets whom one can not help but wish were alive and well. Nakajō Fumiko is one of them. She died in 1954, having lost both breasts to cancer, but were she still living, she would be 71 years old (1993). The collection in which this poem appears was published just before her death. Its tanka sequence "Mourning my breasts" brought her sudden fame just before she died. Love poems extravagant and yet possessed of a cool lucidity, poems of an almost morbid sensitivity, poems of despair about her sickness, poems about her anguish as a mother—she left many different kinds of tanka, and all exhibited her bravery and her talent equally well.

よしあしは
Yoshiashi wa

後の岸の
ushiro no kishi no

人にとへ
hito ni toe

われは颶風に
Ware wa gufū ni

のりて遊べり
norite asoberi

与謝野晶子
Yosano Akiko

Of good and evil
ask them behind
on the shore
As for me, I ride
the storm wind and play

Seigaiha (Blue Waves on the Sea, 1912). With the publication of *Tangled Hair*, Akiko created a sensation and in the following decade became a literary star. Though still in her mid-30s, her poems and essays overflowed with the self-confidence of one who had boldly overcome many obstacles in real life. She also had the pride that comes from being the mother of many children.

Here we have Akiko's self-portrait. The first three lines are provocative, almost defiant, while the last two evoke an image at once dashing and serene. *Gufū*, "storm wind", is a violent, roaring gale. How many writers would be able to imagine, much less say, that riding such a wind is a pleasure?

思ひきや
Omoiki ya

身を浮雲と
Mi wo ukigumo to

なしはてて
nashi hatete

嵐の風に
arashi no kaze ni

まかすべしとは
makasu beshi to wa

崇徳院
Sutoku In

That it should come to this—
Now I am a floating cloud
forced to drift
with storm
and wind
Retired Emperor Sutoku

Hōgen Monogatari. Sutoku, the 75th emperor, began the so-called Hōgen War of 1156 due to a succession dispute, but was defeated and exiled to Sanuki in Shikoku, where he died. A lover of poetry from childhood, he became the author of several famous poems, including one in the *Hyakunin Isshu*. The poem here was written after his defeat, during his house arrest in Kyoto's Ninna Temple. He laments that he has become a floating cloud at the mercy of the storm winds.

Arashi no kaze, translated "storm and wind", is a little redundant, but a poem like this, written, so to speak, on one breath, transcends such technical considerations.

思ひきや
Omoiki ya

ありて忘れぬ
Arite wasurenu

おのが身を
ono ga mi wo

君がかたみに
kimi ga katami ni

なさむものとは
nasamu mono to wa

和泉式部
Izumi Shikibu

That it should come to this—
my own body,
alive and never forgetting,
is all that I have left
of you

Izumi Shikibu Zokushū. Like Emperor Sutoku in the previous poem, Izumi begins with the lament *omoiki ya*, a rhetorical question whose literal meaning is "did I ever expect . . . ?"

Heian court poetry is usually thought to have valued elegance above all, but Ariwara Narihira and Saigyō are two other poets who used this phrase to wonderful effect in some superb poems, which shows that there was also a tradition of strongly emotional language.

Izumi's poem is one of a group expressing her deep despair and grief at the sudden death of Prince Atsumichi, whom she had loved passionately. Your love, she says, is inscribed everywhere on my body, which never forgets, and now my body has become all that I have left of you.

軍神の
Gunshin no

母のひとりが
haha no hitori ga

年老いて
toshi oite

夜はさすがに
yoru wa sasuga ni

さみしといひき
samishi to iiki

半田良平
Handa Ryōhei

A war god's mother
said
"I'm old now
and naturally, the nights
are lonely"

Kōboku, 1948. All three of the author's sons fought and died in the Pacific War, the two oldest of illness and the third in 1944 on Saipan. The group of elegiac tanka at the end of *Kōboku* speak in the grieving voices of parents who lost their sons to war. This poem captures the moment when the true feelings of a mother whose son was one of the many "war gods" (*gunshin*, a title awarded posthumously for bravery) spill over. In spite of her son's commendation for bravery, now she is old, he is gone, and at night she has to face the terrible loneliness of his absence. The deep sympathy that pervades this poem cannot help but move the reader.

白露や

Shiratsuyu ya

死んでゆく日も

Shinde yuku hi mo

帯締めて

obi shimete

三橋鷹女

Mitsuhashi Takajo

White dew . . .
Even on the day I die
I'll wear an obi

Hakkotsu, 1952. The title means "bleached bones". Another of her haiku collections was called *Shida Jigoku*, or "fern hell". The assertive titles suggest what a strongly individual poet she was. But there was another side to her individuality, shown in poems as lean as this one, also from *Hakkotsu*: "My hands and feet, / bleached bone, / quiver as the leaves fall" (*Hakkotsu no teashi ga soyogu rakuyō-ki*).

Takajo confronted death head-on without any self-indulgence. Many of her poems are full of a sense of intensely alive isolation: "In summer I grow thin / but what I hate / I hate" (*Natsu yasete kirai na mono wa kirai nari*), "Everything is dreams / Oh, the primroses / have bloomed" (*Minna yume Yukiwarisō ga saita no ne*). But in "White dew . . . / Even on the day I die / I'll wear an obi", the combination of noble dignity and desolation evokes a grave and serene sadness.

入れ替への
Irekae no

催促に来る
saisoku ni kuru

赤とんぼ
akatonbo

誹風柳多留拾遺
Haifū Yanagidaru Shūi

Come to press me
to redeem my winter clothes—
a red dragonfly

The word *irekae*, literally "replacing", has passed out of our vocabulary today, but in the Edo period it was an essential word in the life of the common people. When autumn arrived, people felt they had to take their winter clothes back from the pawnbroker and pawn their summer ones instead; *irekae* was the name for this process.

Bashō wrote: "Dragonfly ... / Unable to cling / to a blade of grass" (*Tonbō ya Tori-tsuki kaneshi kusa no ue*), and Buson wrote: "Dragonfly ... / The color of the wall / reminds me of home" (*Tonbō ya Mura natsukashiki kabe no iro*). But for *senryū*, or lighthearted haiku, the dragonfly's seasonal associations, as seen here, were quite different.

邂逅を
Kaikō wo

遂げたる夢の
togetaru yume no

腕のなかに
ude no naka ni

光となりて
hikari to narite

われはひろがる
ware wa hirogaru

山本かね子
Yamamoto Kaneko

I dreamt you found me
at last
and in your arms
I turned to light
shed radiance everywhere

Kaze nari, 1972. Born in 1926 in Niigata Prefecture, she studied tanka with Uematsu Hisaki.

From earliest times, the tanka had the power to evoke fragments of a narrative world. The 10th century *Tales of Ise*, which unfolded its stories in a seamless interweave of poetry and prose, was traditionally used as a handbook for poets, but in modern times its narrative aspect has been stressed, as can be seen in the term for it introduced by Kubota Utsubo, which is *utamonogatari*, or "poem tale".

This modern love poem somehow reminds me of the world of Heian period poem-tales like *Tales of Ise*. A woman dreams that she is able at last to meet her lover and within his arms dissolves into radiant light.

たらちねの
Tarachine no

親の守りと
oya no mamori to

相添ふる
ai-souru

心ばかりは
kokoro bakari wa

関な留めそ
seki na todome so

小野千古の母
Ono no Chifuru no Haha

The amulet
I send with my child
is my heart and only that
Let it pass
through all your barriers
The Mother of Ono no Chifuru

Kokinshū, Book 8, Parting. The prefatory note explains that this poem was written by the mother of a government official called Ono no Chifuru, when he was appointed to a post in Michinoku in the far north.

Ancient people believed that the mind could separate from the body. In this poem, the mother says that to protect her child on his long trip, she has separated her heart from her body and sent it with him, as an amulet to ward off evil—so, please, guardians of the barrier, excuse a parent's heart and let it through, even if it does not have a proper pass. A very original poem.

月天心
Tsuki tenshin

貧しき町を
mazushiki machi wo

通りけり
tōri keri

与謝蕪村
Yosa Buson

Moon sky center
I pass
through ghetto streets

Buson Kushū. I first read this haiku in a middle school textbook when I was in my teens, but did not understand it very well. Before learning that *tenshin* meant "in the precise middle of the sky," I had heard of the poet and art critic Okakura Tenshin, whose first name is written with the same characters, and this apparently gave rise to some confusion in my mind. Besides that, I thought that it was the moon itself that was passing through the streets, not the poet. This poem taught me the importance of the break (which here comes after *tsuki tenshin*) in haiku.

世の中は
Yo no naka wa

たゞうたたねの
tada utatane no

しばらくを
shibaraku wo

覚めぬ夢路に
samenu yumeji ni

まどふわりなさ
madou warinasa

太田垣蓮月
Ōtagaki Rengetsu

Life passes quickly
as a little nap, but who can explain
why we spend it wandering
in the world of dreams
and never wake?

Ama no Karumo. A *jukkai* poem, that is, one which expresses the poet's feelings about human life. From olden times, such poems have taken the transience of life as their main subject.

Rengetsu, who took orders as a Buddhist nun after losing four children and her husband to death, became widely known for her pottery and lived until the age of 85. But in her heart she must always have had the feeling expressed in this poem. Life passes with the brevity of a brief sleep, but we pursue only the wandering path of dreams and die without ever waking to the true reality—such, she says, is the inscrutability of human life.

鴨じもの
Kamo jimo no

浮寝をすれば
ukine wo sureba

蜷の腸
mina no wata

か黒き髪に
kaguroki kami ni

露そ置きにける
tsuyu so okinikeru

よみ人しらず
Yomibito shirazu

Like a wild duck
I slept floating on the sea
and on my hair
that is black as snails' innards
the dew settled

Author unknown

Man'yoshū, Volume 15. An unusual volume, it contains 145 poems by the members of a diplomatic mission who sailed to the ancient Korean kingdom of Silla in 736. This tanka was written when the party had been blown off course by a storm.

Kamo jimo no is the modern *kamo no yō ni*, "like a wild duck." *Mina no wata* means the innards of the *mina* (modern *nina*), a small snail. It was used as a pillow word, or ritualized modifier for *kuroki*, "black", probably because the innards turn black when roasted.

There is an immediacy to the poet's perception as, drifting helplessly, he suddenly notices the night dew on his hair. Sometimes the best-remembered things are the little ones.

有明や
Ariake ya

浅間の霧が
Asama no kiri ga

膳をはふ
zen wo hau

小林一茶
Kobayashi Issa

The dawn moon
Fog from Asama drifts
over my breakfast tray

Shichiban Nikki. Ariake can mean the dawn, or the moon still in the sky at dawn; here it means the latter. In olden days, travelers left their inns at daybreak and hurried to their destinations under the dawn moon.

Issa wrote this poem in 1812, when he had to travel back and forth on the Nakasendō highway between Edo and his birthplace Kashiwabara in order to sort out a complicated dispute about his inheritance. He had spent the night at Karuizawa, at the foot of Mt. Asama. Fog from the mountain trailed over the trays set out for the early departing travelers' breakfasts. The scene is refreshing, but at the same time the fog seems to reflect the cloud over Issa's heart.

手を切れ、
Te wo kire,

雙脚を切れ、
moroashi wo kire,

野のつちに投げ棄てておけ、
no no tsuchi ni nagesutete oke,

秋と親しまむ
aki to shitashimamu

若山牧水
Wakayama Bokusui

*Cut off these hands, cut off these feet,
throw them out on the wild earth
I want to be alone with autumn*

Shi ka geijutsu ka (Death or Art?, 1912). Bokusui's next tanka collection, *Minakami* (The River's Source, 1913), also had many poems which burst the bounds of the tanka's regular form. For example: "My life force shines, / oiled to a damp, black sheen; / as if it had / not yet known / fire..." (*Waga seizonryoku wa, imada hi wo shirazaru gotoshi, abura ni kuroku nurete kagayakedo*). In the background was a tortured love affair and its aftermath of extreme depression, as well as the suffering due to the death of his father and uncertainty about his own future. The formal irregularity had an inner necessity. And yet, the last line emerges with lyrical grace.

なにとなく
Nani to naku

君に待たるる
kimi ni mataruru

ここちして
kokochi shite

出でし花野の
ideshi hanano no

夕月夜かな
yūzukuyo kana

与謝野晶子
Yosano Akiko

Somehow feeling
you awaited me,
I went into
the flowering meadow
under the evening moon

Midaregami, 1901. Many people tend to think of *hanano* as spring meadows, but in haiku, *hanano* is an autumn word for meadows full of wildflowers. It is hard to tell, though, whether Akiko was thinking of spring or autumn in this tanka. Even in her own commentary on the poem, she did not touch on the question.

The poem dates from when she was still the unmarried Hō Shō, living in her parents' home in Sakai, near Osaka. Is the "you" of the poem a man like Prince Genji, appearing in her virginal fantasies? An elegant and charming poem, with a faint but unmistakable air of self-adoration.

おもひ切たる
Omoikittaru

死ぐるひ見よ
shinigurui miyo

史邦
Fumikuni

Look at that man fight,
mad for death!

青天に
Seiten ni

有明月の
ariakezuki no

朝ぼらけ
asaborake

去来
Kyorai

Against azure skies,
the morning moon
It's daybreak

湖水の秋の
Kosui no aki no

比良のはつ霜
Hira no hatsu-
shimo

芭蕉
Bashō

Autumn on the lake:
Hira's first frosts

From "The Kite's Feathers", a sequence of *The Monkey's Raincoat*. Fumikuni's link, lacking a season word, is of the "miscellaneous" category; the other two are autumn.

Read consecutively, the three links evoke a sense of sharp, bracing purity. The desperate fight of a warrior resolved to die is juxtaposed with the dawn sky as it clears, revealing a faint morning moon. Around Lake Biwa autumn is deepening, Mount Hira already touched by the first frosts. This is the unique world of linked verse, where nature and human beings are newly and dramatically combined.

風きけば
Kaze kikeba

嶺の木の葉の
mine no konoha no

中空に
nakazora ni

吹き捨てられて
fuki suterarete

落つる声々
otsuru koegoe

正徹
Shōtetsu

I hear the wind
in the mountain trees
and the voices of the leaves
blown through air
then let go, falling

Sōkonshū. Shōtetsu, a Buddhist priest and lead-
ing tanka poet of the early Muromachi period, was
born in the province of Bitchū, the son of the lord
of Kōdoyama (Okayama Prefecture). When he was
about 10, he and his parents moved to Kyoto. By
his teens, he was participating in tanka workshops
held by recognized poets in Kyoto. He later took
monastic vows, but continued to be active as a poet
and critic and took many renga poets, including
Shinkei, under his wing. He is an excellent example
of the many poet-priests of the Muromachi period.
A prolific poet, he is said to have written 40,000
tanka. As this poem shows, his style, with its close
attention to such subtle events as the far-off sound
of the wind, was capable of creating deep over-
tones.

月読は
Tsukiyomi wa

光澄みつつ
hikari sumitsutsu

外に坐せり
to ni maseri

かく思ふ我や
Kaku omou ware ya

水の如かる
mizu no gotokaru

北原白秋
Kitahara Hakushū

The moon god's light
outside
is bright and clear
And I who think this
am like water

Kurohi (Black Cypress, 1940). From early autumn of 1937, Hakushū had been losing his sight, due to kidney disease and diabetes, the diseases of which he died in 1942. *Kurohi*, published two and a half years after he became ill, has many poems about his dimming sight. It is also one of the best collections of his later years.

Tsukiyomi has come to mean the moon, but originally meant the moon deity. Here the feeling of the word is close to its original meaning. Sitting indoors late at night, the poet thinks of the moonlight outside. A person who sees only dimly envisions the moonlight more and more clearly within the heart. The last two lines, with their quietness, evoke an altered state of mind.

薄紅葉
Usumomiji

恋人ならば
Koibito naraba

烏帽子で来
eboshi de ko

三橋鷹女
Mitsuhashi Takajo

Pale maple leaves
If you're to be my lover
come in a high silk hat

Uo no Hire, 1941. When I like a poem, I find myself imagining what the author is like, even how she or he looks. This is one of the pleasures of reading that everyone must have experienced at one time or another, and Takajo is a haiku poet who often inspires it.

Gazing at the maple leaves just begining to redden, Takajo, in a daring burst of anachronism, orders her lover to come to her wearing an ancient *eboshi* hat. Her voice is soft, almost as if talking to herself, and her tone combines lofty refinement with a high-spirited young woman's playful sensuality.

The *eboshi* or "crow hat" (translated freely as "a high silk hat") derives its name from the crow, often used as a simile for blackness in classical Japanese literature. It was worn by adult males beginning in the Nara period.

円光を
Enkō wo

著て鴛鴦の
kite oshidori no

目をつむり
me wo tsumuri

長谷川素逝
Hasegawa Sosei

Wrapped in light
the mandarin ducks
shut their eyes

Rekijitsu, **1946.** Mandarin ducks floating on a pond have an attention-arresting beauty and charm unique even among water birds. Here they are resting on the water, the light encircling their bodies like a nimbus. The line *me wo tsumuri* ("shut their eyes") brings the scene's lonely purity into perfect focus. This is how a simple description of nature can become at the same time an expression of the poet's emotion.

Sosei was on a poem-writing trip, though gravely ill, when he saw these ducks in the Outer Gardens of Ise Shrine. He wrote other superb poems on the same trip, and shortly after died.

こしかたゆくすゑ

Koshikata yukusue

雪あかりする

Yuki akari suru

種田山頭火

Taneda Santōka

The past, the future—
snowlight faintly glows

Sōmokutō, 1940. After a troubled and stormy youth, Santōka in middle age became a Buddhist priest. From 1925 until shortly before he died in 1940, he roamed Japan as a begging monk. This haiku, titled "Return", is from mid-December, 1939, when he had finally settled down in Matsuyama City in a little house he called "A Blade of Grass". The past and the future, it hints, are bathed in unfathomable mystery, but a faint light shines on both, like the dim glow given off by snow at night. Ten months after moving into A Blade of Grass, Santōka died.

孤り棲む
Hitori sumu

埋火の美の
uzumibi no bi no

きはまれり
kiwamareri

竹下しづの女
Takeshita Shizunojo

I live alone
The beauty of the buried embers
is absolute

Teihon Takeshita Shizunojo Kubunshū, 1964. Kyushu has given birth to several prominent female haiku poets—Shizuno-jo, Hisajo, Teijo. Shizunojo had a straight-forward and intellectual style which sometimes led critics to characterize her as "mannish". However, she also wrote poems like this one, which seems to have welled up from the depths of lonely hours of silent contemplation.

Shizunojo's hushand died young, and her oldest son died as he was on his way to becoming a promising haiku poet. In her solitude, the embers dimly visible beneath the ashes take on an extraordinary clarity and beauty. And also loneliness.

すでにすでに
Sude ni sude ni

冬日を鼻に
fuyuhi wo hana ni

おん屍
onkabane

石塚友二
Ishizuka Tomoji

So soon, so soon
the winter sun on its nose—
my teacher's corpse

Kōjin, 1954. In late 1947, the novelist Yokomitsu Riichi died. Tomoji, a writer of fiction and haiku, had been his follower. This is one of several haiku of mourning he wrote under the title "In this world, I have no teacher" (*Konjō ni shi nashi*).

The winter sun is striking nostrils which breathed in and out for nearly 50 years; the person has already become a corpse. With a sense of tragic realization, the poem grasps that solemn instant when life crosses the border into death. I am reminded of Iida Dakotsu's memorable haiku: "Dead body— / Autumn breezes blow / through its nostrils" (*Nakigara ya Akikaze kayou hana no ana*).

年の夜や
Toshi no yo ya

吉野見て来た
Yoshino mite kita

檜笠
hinokigasa

坪井杜国
Tsuboi Tokoku

Tonight the year ends . . .
And there's the cypress hat
that saw Yoshino with me

Oi no Nikki. On the last night of the year, Tokoku notices his traveling hat, made of cypress wickerwork, hanging on the wall. He had worn it when he went to Yoshino to view the cherry blossoms. Looking at it now, the memories of that time return.

Tokoku, a wealthy rice merchant of Nagoya, was one of Bashō's favorite disciples. It was Bashō who had invited him to Yoshino as a way to ease him out of a deep depression. Two years after their trip, the young and handsome disciple, full of nostalgia for the master he adored, wrote this poem about the cypress hat. Several months later he died, and the master in his turn wept.

春立つや
Haru tatsu ya

新年ふるき
Shinnen furuki

米五升
kome goshō

松尾芭蕉
Matsuo Bashō

Spring's begun—
Here's the new year, and a peck
of last year's rice

In the lunar calendar, the new year came later than it does now, and coincided with the first faint stirrings of spring. Bashō wrote this new year's poem when he lived in a cottage in Fukagawa in Edo (now Tokyo). At the time, according to his disciples, his little house held only 10 rice bowls, one knife and a big gourd the disciples had given him. The gourd held exactly one peck of rice.

Furuki kome (literally, "old rice") means the rice given Bashō near the end of the year. With all the rice in my gourd, he thinks, the new year is off to a good start. The contrast between "new" and "old" in the phrase *Shinnen furuki*, and his satisfaction with a mere peck of rice, evoke the humor and elegance of Bashō's own unique vision of monastic poverty.

楽しみ尽きて
Tanoshimi tsukite

哀しみ来る
kanashimi kitaru

天人もなほ五衰の日に逢へり
Tennin mo nao gosui no hi ni aeri

大江朝綱
Ōe no Asatsuna

Pleasure dies
then sadness walks in
And even angels, too, decay

Wakan Rōeishū, Book 2, Mortality. A poem about the view of mortality given voice in such Buddhist expressions as *gosui*, "the five decays", or *tennin gosui*, "the angel's five decays". All that lives must die. Even the angels who know celestial joy exhibit the five signs of decay when it is time for their lives to end. Their beautiful flowery crowns wither and droop, their clothes turn dirty with grime; sweat pours from their armpits, their bodies give off foul odors; and they feel discontented wherever they are. This concept of the decay of the angel influenced later ages in various ways.

牡蠣の口
Kaki no kuchi

もし開かば月
moshi akaba tsuki

さし入らむ
sashiiramu

加藤楸邨
Katō Shūson

If the oyster's mouth

opened

the moon would pour in

Dotō (Raging Seas, 1986). The headnote to this haiku explains that it was inspired by the haiku Hagiwara Sakutarō wrote for the beginning of *Hyōtō*, the last collection of his free verse published in his lifetime. Hagiwara's poem goes like this: "The winter sun has sunk / Remember the oysters / on the rocks!" (*Fuyuhi kurenu Omoiokoseya Iwa ni kaki*). Hagiwara's gray and desolate poem evokes a purely imaginary landscape. Shūson's, in contrast, is a typical example of his unique phantasmic world populated by real creatures.

Let me in turn, inspired by the strange beauty of Shūson's poem, add my own, not 5-7-5 syllables like his, but 7-7, like the second link of a *renku* sequence: "Ring out loud and clear, / oyster tongues and ocean tides" (*Rinrinto nare Shita mo ushio mo*).

一人は
Ichinin wa

なほよしものを
nao yoshi Mono wo

思へるが
omoeru ga

二人あるより
futari aru yori

悲しきは無し
kanashiki wa nashi

与謝野晶子
Yosano Akiko

Brooding's best done
alone
Nothing's sadder
than indulging
together

The first tanka of *Shundeishū* (Spring Thaw, 1911). Akiko's poetry compels by its intellectual power, which brought her overflowing imagination and explosive emotions to heel in the real world as she knew it. Through her married life with Hiroshi, which was far from easy, she apparently developed the strength to look without flinching at the complexities of sexual relationships.

When brooding, it would be easier to be alone; but here are two people brooding together, and there's nothing sadder than that. A poem that makes one think deeply about human life.

ものの行
Mono no yuki

とどまらめやも
todomarame yamo

山峡の
Yamakai no

杉のたいぼくの
sugi no taiboku no

寒さのひびき
samusa no hibiki

斎藤茂吉
Saitō Mokichi

The going of things: does it ever stop?
Great cypresses
between the mountains
their coldness
echoing

Aratama (Uncut Gems, 1921). *Aratama* was Mokichi's second tanka collection after the critically-acclaimed *Shakkō* (Crimson Light, 1913), and with its intense, almost unbreathing scrutiny of the hushed silence at the heart of the natural universe, it became a turning point in the evolution of his poetic voice. Mokichi's theory of composition continued to take shape in tandem with such developments in his practice. He called his theory *shasei*, or natural description, and said it was "To see into actuality with the mind's eye and describe the unitary life of nature and self."

I take the first three lines of this poem as a restatement of the Buddhist idea that all living things must die and be transformed; but the deep quiet the poem projects is Mokichi's own.

最澄の
Saichō no

瞑目つづく
meimoku tsuzuku

冬の畦
Fuyu no aze

宇佐美魚目
Usami Gyomoku

Saichō
still deep in meditation
Winter path

Shūshū Tōzō, 1975. A narrow grass path between wide and withered rice fields in winter. Amidst the spreading silence, the meditating figure of Saichō, or Dengyō Daishi, founder of the Tendai sect of Buddhism, is dimly visible. There is a leap in association from the meditating priest to the winter fields, but it works perfectly, probably because there is an inner necessity in the way the three elements—Saichō, meditation, and a winter path—are linked. No need to imagine a scene out of the ancient Heian period. Now, before our very eyes, Saichō's meditation continues.

きくときに
Kiku toki ni

わが血は騒ぐ
waga chi wa sawagu

鶏の
Niwatori no

卵を生みし
tamago wo umishi

あとを鳴く声
ato wo naku koe

長沢美津
Nagasawa Mitsu

At the sound, my blood leaps—
the hen's cry
after she lays an egg

Kumo wo yobu (I Call the Clouds, 1950). There are literary works which make men and women read them differently. When I read this poem, I can't help wondering if a man would feel this excited when he heard the hen's loud cry after laying an egg. I suspect the author was able to experience this instant of emotion because she is female.

Nagasawa Mitsu was active in the formation of the Women's Tanka Association just after World War II, and more recently completed the enormous task of compiling and editing the six-volume *Compendium of Women's Waka*.

水に浮く
Mizu ni uku

柄杓の上の
hishaku no ue no

春の雪
haru no yuki

高浜虚子
Takahama Kyoshi

Spring snow
atop a ladle
floating on water

Gohyakku, 1937. Kyoshi's haiku often offer a sudden glimpse of large worlds through a concentration on small things. There is, for example, his "So much depends / on the coming into bud / of things" (*Mono no me no araware ideshi daiji kana*). And also: "How quiet / is the sound / of a butterfly eating" (*Chō chō no mono kuu oto no shizukasa yo*), "A single pawlonia leaf, / bathed in sunlight, / fell" (*Kiri hitoha hi atarinagara ochinike-ri*), "The snake fled, / its eyes that saw me / left behind in the grass" (*Hebi nigete ware wo mishi me no kusa ni nokoru*).

This haiku is of the same sort. A floating ladle is light to begin with, the soft spring snow piled on top of it lighter still. And what the poem points us to is all of spring itself.

紅白の
Kōhaku no

梅の匂ひを
ume no nioi wo

嗅ぎ分けて
kagiwakete

いひ知れぬ今日の
iishirenu kyō no

喜びにをり
yorokobi ni ori

坂田泡光
Sakata Hōkō

Today
I can tell
the red plum and the white
by their scent—
no words for this joy

Mōjō, 1986. A Christian poet who developed Hansen's disease in his teens and spent over fifty years in a sanitarium. Because of his illness, both eyes had to be surgically removed. He has also written: "My sense of smell restored, / in joy now / I come / to the grove of plum / in full bloom" (*Kyūkaku no modorikitarishi yorokobi ni ima mankai no bairin ni kitsu*), "Again I've returned / to a world / which has no smell / and the spirea, they say, / is in full bloom" (*Nioi shiranu sekai ni mata mo modoritari Yukiyanagi no hana sakari to iu ni*).

To someone who has suffered the loss of the senses of smell and touch it becomes "a joy" for which there are "no words" to be able to know the difference between the scents of pink plum blossoms and white ones.

わがこころ
Waga kokoro

しづかならざる
shizuka narazaru

ときにきて
toki ni kite

語りつくせよ
kataritsukuse yo

遠き世のこと
Tōki yo no koto

山中智恵子
Yamanaka Chieko

At times when my heart
is unquiet
come and tell me
every single thing you have to tell
about that long-lost world

Seishi, 1984. The poet is speaking to her husband, who is dead. "At the bottom / of this night's sleep / you will come / sometime, / become one of the gentle dead" (*Kono yoru no nemuri no soko ni itsuka kite yasashiki shisha to kimi naritamō*). Shortly after the poet lost her husband, with whom she had lived for thirty years, she wrote a tremendous number of poems of mourning in a very short time. The poem above does not express her grief directly, but the grief hidden within its quiet tenderness is all the more moving for that. The poem turns, as it were, into a collaboration with the man it mourns.

空青く
Sora aoku

雀よく鳴き
suzume yoku naki

タンポポの
tanpopo no

日毎に咲けば
higoto ni sakeba

わが春たのし
waga haru tanoshi

林　圭子
Hayashi Keiko

Blue sky
    the sparrows chirping
        dandelions blooming
every day
    My spring is glad

Mejirodai, 1985. This was her fourth volume of tanka. Tsuzuki Shōgo wrote this preface poem for it: "Many are the works / which help to understand / Utsubo / but the ones I will not forget / are Keiko's tanka" (*Utsubo kenkyū shiryō kusagusa amata aredo wasuremajiki wa Keiko shoka-shū*).

Hayashi Keiko was married to Kubota Utsubo, a leading modern tanka poet. Born in the 29th year of the Meiji period, 1896, she died in 1989, over 90. She wrote this poem when she was 87. Reading it with that knowledge, I am amazed at its unself-conscious sense of freedom.

"I remember / the full moon, / how my husband's hand on his pipe / vividly floated up / in its light" (*Kiseru motsu tsuma no temoto no azaya-ka ni hikari ni ukishi meigetsu omou*). Such poems must come from a kind of lonely serenity.

木の間なる
Ko no ma naru

染井吉野の
somei yoshino no

白ほどの
shiro hodo no

はかなき命
hakanaki inochi

抱く春かな
idaku haru kana

与謝野晶子
Yosano Akiko

It is spring
and I embrace a life
frail as the whiteness
of cherry blossoms
among the trees

Hakuōshū (White Cherry Blossoms, 1942). When Akiko's husband, Hiroshi, died in March 1935, Akiko wrote: "This world was too harsh for you / but you were not bitter, / you said nothing. . . / Like a mountain / in majesty you endured" (*Tsurakarishi Yo wo mo uramazu iwazu shite yama no gotoku ni imashitsuru kimi*). Akiko's solitude and loneliness after Hiroshi's death were intense. She herself died of illness seven years later.

The poem above was written in 1940, while she was convalescing from a cerebral hemorrhage. It evokes tremendous sadness, but the tone is totally self-possesed.

She also wrote: "Let me die / thinking I hold / a vial / of the elixir / of immortality" (*Mizukara wa fushi no kusuri no tsubo idaku mi to omoitsutsu shinan to suran*). This great poet had arrived at a serene, unblinking self-knowledge that is reflected directly in the world of her poetry.

父君に
Chichigimi ni

召されていなむ
mesarete inamu

とこしへの
Tokoshie no

春あたゝかき
haru atatakaki

蓬莱のしま
Hōrai no shima

山川登美子
Yamakawa Tomiko

My father calls
and I shall go
Warm Hōrai Island
where spring
is eternal

Yamakawa Tomiko Zenshū, edited by Sakamoto Masaki, Vol. 1, 1972. The deathbed poem of a tanka poet who died when she was barely 29, on April 15, 1909. Two days before her death, she wrote this on rolled letter-paper and gave it to her younger brother Ryōzō.

Respected as highly as Yosano Akiko in the *Myōjō* group of poets, Tomiko was born into the family of a hereditary high-ranking vassal of the old Obama fief and grew up bearing on her shoulders the dreams of her father Teizō, a proponent of education for women. Here, in her last moments, about to leave this world, she writes of her dream of staying forever with her dead father on Hōrai, the island of eternal youth.

菫咲く
Sumire saku

春は夢殿
haru wa Yumedono

日おもてを
Hi omote wo

石段の目に
ishikida no me ni

乾く埴土
kawaku hanitsuchi

北原白秋
Kitahara Hakushū

Violets bloom   It's spring at Yumedono
In the clefts of sunlit stone steps
the dry henna-colored earth

Yumedono, 1939. This is not a poem which moves smoothly along, saying all it has to say in one breath. I suspect that what Hakushū wanted to convey by writing about Hōryūji's Yumedono was no more and no less than the experience of encountering spring in the ancient capital of Nara. That is why he tried very hard to convey the physical sensation of the stone steps warmed by the sun and the dry, reddish-yellow earth in their cracks—a very small sensation, but once you notice it, redolent of the feeling of spring in the ancient capital.

花を踏みし
Hana wo fumishi

草履も見えて
zōri mo miete

朝寝哉
asane kana

与謝蕪村
Yosa Buson

Some sandals walked
on flowers, I see...
Morning sleep

Buson Kushū. "Visiting the inn in Kiyamachi where someone from Naniwa was staying," says the preface note. Buson paid a call on a friend from Osaka who was staying at an inn in Kiyamachi, which is on the Kamo River in Kyoto. Among the sandals lined up at the entrance were some with flower petals stuck to them, left from tramping about viewing the cherry blossoms until late the night before. The inn was dead silent, the guests sleeping in.

Though unrelated to economic activity, flower-viewing and other elegant pursuits had an indirect but crucial link to the prosperity of the Kyoto region.

Supplementary

Glossary

Where the term is the name of a poetic genre, examples of that genre are indexed following the definition.

Chinese poetry, see *kanshi*.

crazy poems, see *kyōka*.

folk songs. 43, 56, 63, 76, 97, 119, 129

free-verse. 7, 30, 31, 88, 99, 104

fuzoku-uta. Provincial folk songs from Heian and earlier eras, often sung at banquets. 43, 97.

gogon zekku (five-word quatrain). A Chinese poem of four lines, five Chinese characters each. See also *kanshi* and *shichigon risshi*. 11, 21

Gosechi song. One of the lyrics sung during the Gosechi Festivals of the Heian court, held each winter. 50

gozan bungaku (five-mountain literature). Writings of the Zen monks of the five large Rinzai temples of Kamakura and Kyoto, flourished 14th-16th centuries. 92

haikai (humorous). In the *Kokinshū*, a category of *tanka*. Since the Edo Period, mainly refers to *haikai no renga*, the popular style of linked-verse practiced by Bashō and his followers. 22, 28, 69, 71, 74, 87, 103, 106, 148, 159

haiku (literally: stanza of *haikai*). A traditional poem typically in three lines of five, seven, and five syllables and including a "season word" (*kigo*). In the latter half of the twentieth century haiku has become a world-wide genre, adapted into many different languages. 2, 4, 5, 6, 8, 10, 17, 34, 37, 38, 41, 45, 49, 52, 53, 58, 62, 69, 71, 77, 79, 81, 82, 94, 96, 101, 108, 110, 111, 113, 114, 117, 118, 121, 122, 125, 130, 138, 142, 145, 151, 152, 153, 154, 155, 156, 157, 159, 162, 164, 171

jōruri (pure lapis lazuli). A ballad-drama, presented in the puppet theater. Also called *bunraku*. Named after Princess Jōruri, heroine of early dramatic narratives.

jukkai (to speak feelings). One of the classical topics in *waka*: a poem expressing one's feelings, usually of personal "grievance". 143

kagura uta (song to amuse the gods). The lyrics of *kagura*, sacred dances at Shinto shrines held from ancient times and continuing today. 3

kanshi (Chinese poem). A poem written in classical Chinese. Such poems are usually read in an inflected Japanese translation, such as those given here. See also *gogon zekku* and *shichigon risshi*. 11, 21, 42, 63, 67, 73, 80, 91, 92, 95, 127, 158

kyōka (crazy poem). A poem in *tanka* form, written with humorous intent. 44, 105, 126

linked poem, linked verse, see *renga*, and *haikai*.

literary language, poem in. 115

Nakamabushi (Nakama song). A group of songs from Okinawa. 25

omoro. Sacred songs of prayer from Okinawa, sometimes narrative, with varied form and content. They flourished from the 12th to the early 17th centuries. 24

popular song, 86, 89

pre-modern song, 26, 39

provincial folk songs, see *fuzoku-uta*.

renga (linked poem). Refers to a wide variety of traditional Japanese poems, usually written by two or more poets in collaboration. The classic form is a long poem, usually of one hundred stanzas but sometimes reaching a thousand or more, that flourished during the Muromachi period. 64

renku (linked verse). Modern term for *haikai*, which see.

ryūka (Ryukyu song). The *tanka* of Okinawa and the Ryukyu Islands. Composed in thirty syllables arranged 8-8-8-6, it was a lyrical form, often about love, and sung to samisan accompaniment. 25

satiric verse, see *kyōka* and *senryū*.

sedōka (repeated-head poem). A poem of two verses of 5, 7, and 7 syllables each. Found almost exclusively in the *Manyōshū*. 112

senryū (river willow). A humorous verse in *haiku* form. The word is the pen-name of a renowned master of the genre. 139

shichigon risshi (seven-word poem). A Chinese poem of seven Chinese characters per line, the standard length being eight lines. See also *gogon zekku* and *kanshi*. 92, 95

Shinto song, see *kagura uta*.

tanka (short poem). The classic Japanese poem, a lyric in five lines typically of five, seven, five, seven, and seven syllables. See also *kyōka*. 1, 9, 13, 14, 15, 16, 18, 19, 20, 23, 27, 29, 32, 33, 35, 36, 40, 46, 47, 48, 49, 51, 54, 55, 57, 59, 60, 61, 65, 66, 68, 70, 72, 75, 78, 83, 85, 90, 93, 98, 100, 102, 107, 109, 116, 120, 123, 124, 128, 131, 132, 133, 134, 135, 136, 137, 140, 141, 143, 144, 146, 147, 149, 150, 160, 161, 163, 165, 166, 167, 168, 169, 170

translation, 12, 84

utamonogatari (poem-tale). A sequence of *tanka* with context-setting prose, each paired preface and poem taken together as a narrative unit. 140

waka (Japanese poem/poetry). A general term for traditional Japanese poetry, today usually synonymous with *tanka*, but sometimes including *chōka*, *sedōka*, and other traditional poems written in native Japanese.

wild *tanka*, see *kyōka*.

Index of First Lines, Japanese

In addition to the first lines in romanized Japanese, titles are given here if they appear in the text. A title is indicated by quotation marks.

Index of First Lines, English

In addition to the first lines of the English translations, translated titles are given here if they appear in the text. A title is indicated by quotation marks.

Index of Authors

If the author is unknown this index lists the title of the source. Thus, an anonymous poem from the *Kokinshū* is listed under *Kokinshū*, but other *Kokinshū* poems by known authors are listed only by authors.

The possessive particle *no* which appears optionally in many names is usually omitted in this index.

Page numbers in italics indicate literary persons mentioned in the text, often as teachers or influences.

ŌOKA MAKOTO

Ōoka Makoto was born February 16, 1931, in Shizuoka, Japan. His father was an educator and *tanka* poet.

On graduating from the Tokyo University Department of Literature in 1953, he joined the Yomiuri Newspapers as a reporter. He taught Japanese literature at Meiji University 1965-87. From 1988 until 1993 he was Professor of Japanese Literature at the National University of Fine Arts and Music.

Ōoka is the author of 19 books of poetry. His 15-volume collectedworks were published 1974-75.

Among Ōoka's 200 published books are plays and movie scripts, as well as volumes on art criticism, poetics, literary criticism, and classic poetry.

Ōoka Makoto's writings have earned him a number of honors and awards. Chief among them:

1969:	Rekitei Prize for poetic theory (*A Family of Prodigal Sons: The Path of Modern Japanese Poetry*)
1972:	Yomiuri Prize for literary criticism (*Ki no Tsurayuki*)
1979:	Mugen Prize for Poetry (*For a Girl in Spring*)
1980:	Kikuchi Kan Prize for cross-disciplinary achievements (*Occasional Verses*)
1989:	Shiseido Hanatsubaki Prize for Poetry (*Messages to the Water in My Hometown*)
1990:	Education Minister's Prize of the Art Commendation of Japan (*Sugawara Michizane as Poet*)
1993:	Prize of the Museum of Contemporary Japanese Poetry, Tanka, and Haiku (*Afternoon of the Terrestrial Paradise*)
1993:	Culture Prize of the Municipality of Tokyo

Many of Ōoka Makoto's books have been translated, and his selected poems have appeared in Chinese, Dutch, English, French, and German, while linked poems on which he has collaborated have appeared in Dutch, English, Estonian, Finnish, and German.

Ōoka Makoto served as president of the Japan PEN Club from 1989 to 1993. In 1993 he was made *Officier de l'Ordre des Arts et des Lettres* by the French government.

JANINE BEICHMAN

Janine Beichman was born and educated in the United States, and received her doctorate in East Asian Studies from Columbia University. She has lived in Japan since 1969, lectured at Sophia University and is associate professor of Japanese literature at Daitō Bunka University.

She has studied Noh chanting and written an original English-language Noh play, *Drifting Fires*, which has been produced in Japan and the United States. She has also written tanka and critical articles published in Japanese.

Beichman's publications in English include *Masaoka Shiki*, a literary biography, and translations, articles, and reviews in such journals as *Monumenta Nipponica, Japan Quarterly,* and *Proceedings of the National Institute of Japanese Literature.* She is currently completing a biography of the modern poet Yosano Akiko, part of which was written while a fellow of the National Endowment for the Humanities in 1991-1992.

Asian Poetry in Translation: Japan

Editor, Thomas Fitzsimmons

#1 *Devil's Wind: A Thousand Steps*, Yoshimasu Gozo

#2 *Sun, Sand and Wind*, Shozu Ben

#3 *A String Around Autumn: Selected Poems 1952-1980*,
   Ōoka Makoto

#4 *Treelike: The Poetry of Kinoshita Yuji*
   —Japan-US Friendship Commission Translation Prize

#5 *Dead Languages: Selected Poems 1946-1984*, Tamura Ryuichi

#6 *Celebration in Darkness: Selected Poems of Yoshioka Minoru* &
   Strangers' Sky: Selected Poems of Iijima Koichi

#7 *A Play of Mirrors: Eight Major Poets of Modern Japan*, anthology

#8 *A Thousand Steps . . . and More: Selected Poems and Prose 1964-
   1984*, Yoshimasu Gozo

#9 *Demented Flute: Selected Poems 1967-1986*, Sasaki Mikiro

#10 *I Am Alive: The Tanka Poems of Goto Miyoko*

#11 *Moonstone Woman: Selected Poems and Prose*, Tada Chimako

#12 *Self-Righting Lamp: Selected Poems*, Maruyama Kaoru

#13 *Mt. Fuji: Selected Poems 1943-1986*, Kusano Shinpei

#14 *62 Sonnets and Definitions*, Tanikawa Shuntaro

#15 *The New Poetry of Japan—the 70s and 80s*, anthology

Supported by the National Endowment for the Arts, the Japan-US Friendship Commission, Oakland University (MI), University of Michigan Center for Japanese Studies, the Saison Cultural Foundation (Japan), the University of Sydney (Australia), and UNESCO.

Reflections

Editor, Thomas Fitzsimmons

The Colors of Poetry: Essays on Classic Japanese Verse, Ōoka Makoto

Haiku: Messages from Matsuyama, Yagi Kametaro

A Poet's Anthology: The Range of Japanese Poetry, Ōoka Makoto

Water Ground Stone, Thomas Fitzsimmons and Karen Hargreaves-Fitzsimmons

Stages and Views, Penny Harter